A 52-Week Experience on Investing in Love for a Lifetime Return

MARRIAGE EQUITY

DEVOTIONAL

JOHN AND SANDRA POSEY

© 2019 The Preachers Trainer Inc

All rights reserved. No portion of this book may be reproduced, stored in a retrieval system, or transmitted in any form or by any means—electronic, mechanical, photocopy, recording, scanning, or other—except for brief quotations in critical reviews or articles, without the prior written permission of the publisher.

Published by The Preachers Trainer Inc

ISBN: 978-1-7337959-0-6

Scripture quotations marked (AMPC) are from the Amplified Bible Classic Edition. Copyright © 1954, 1958, 1962, 1964, 1965, 1987 by The Lockman Foundation. Used by permission (www.lockman.org).

Scripture quotations marked (ESV) are from the The Holy Bible, English Standard Version. ESV® Text Edition: 2016. Copyright © 2001 by Crossway Bibles, a publishing ministry of Good News Publishers.

Scripture quotations marked (KJV) are from the King James Version (public domain).

Scripture quotations marked (GNT) are from the Good News Translation® (Today's English Version, Second Edition) Copyright © 1992 American Bible Society. All rights reserved.

Scripture quotations marked (The Message) are from The Message. Copyright © 1993, 1994, 1995, 1996, 2000, 2001, 2002. Used by permission of NavPress Publishing Group.

Scripture quotations marked (NET Bible) are from the NET Bible® copyright ©1996-2006 by Biblical Studies Press, L.L.C. http://netbible.com. All rights reserved.

Scripture quotations marked (NIV) are from THE HOLY BIBLE, NEW INTERNATIONAL VERSION®, NIV® Copyright © 1973, 1978, 1984, 2011 by Biblica, Inc.® Used by permission. All rights reserved worldwide.

Scripture quotations marked (NKJV) are from the New King James Version®. Copyright © 1982 by Thomas Nelson. Used by permission. All rights reserved.

Scripture quotations marked (NLT) are from Holy Bible, New Living Translation, copyright © 1996, 2004, 2015 by Tyndale House Foundation. Used by permission of Tyndale House Publishers, Inc., Carol Stream, Illinois 60188. All rights reserved.

Scripture quotations marked (WEB) are from the World English Bible (public domain).

Copy Editing and Interior Layout: James Armstrong, UpWrite Publishing

Cover Design: Michael Sean Allen and Scott Rasmussen

April 2019 Edition

Endorsements

I love John and Sandra Posey's new *Marriage Equity Systems Devotional*! This marriage resource is long overdue. The way that John and Sandra incorporate Bible truths with practicalities of marriage is sure to be an amazing help to any married couple. The grace and gifting of both of them can clearly be seen in these pages.

My dear husband, Tim, has said that he appreciates ideas of ways to be more romantic, to bless me, and this is an amazing supply. I am sure all husbands and wives feel similarly to some extent, and this source will be a great enrichment in their three-fold marriage union through the Poseys' carefully laid out devotional.

This material will be such a powerful tool to begin marriages, to help correct marriages, and to be a keepsake in homes, cherished and shared among families, friends, and acquaintances. I know for us, this will be stocked in our ministry offices for gifts and reference for many ways to help marriages.

"Keeping it real" is who we have found John and Sandra to be after these many years of ministry, friendship and close family involvement. Tim and I have always appreciated their being strong examples, giving attention to keeping purposeful focus on their marriage.

I see this devotional playing an important part as God revives marriages in the Body of Christ and directs marriages toward a healthier, more loving, and more successful experience within the church of our Lord Jesus Christ.

Kristeen Mann
Director, Church Builders International
Pastor, The Surge Church

***

Allow me a few moments to share with you my thoughts on John and Sandra Posey's new *Marriage Equity System Devotional.*

My first thought is WOW! They have captured the essence of living in a happy, successful marriage, and they are sharing it with us in these 52 lessons. Their thoughts are not just sermons, but practical applications born out of decades of practice and success. Certainly, the Biblical thoughts are presented as a foundation, but then they show us how to apply the Scriptures in our own daily lives.

As fellow ministers and close family friends, Kris and I have seen for 32 years firsthand how they apply these principles, and they are shining examples to us on how to live as "One Flesh" and enjoy it.

You can't go wrong following their wisdom!

Timothy Mann
Founder and President, Church Builders International

***

John and Sandra have provided a transparent, relevant look into what it takes to make a marriage work. The concepts presented are simplistic yet profoundly effective when followed. John and Sandra's stories provide a pathway around many relationship land mines. The affirmations provide an immediate opportunity to begin the required adjustments. There is a consistent thread of relationship equality between husband and wife presented throughout each chapter. This is a significant concept for young and mature marriages alike.

Kenneth Hill
President, The Launchpad Foundation

***

Buckle your seat belts. It's quite a ride. John and Sandra Posey invite you into their lives to see how two flawed people (like you and me) are learning to love each other as an extension of their love for God.

From the first week to the last they share God's Word, God's heart, and God's purpose in and through marriage. If you know John and Sandra, you won't be surprised. If you don't know them, you will discover they are the real deal. They practice what they preach, and they model what they teach. John and Sandra's 52-week marriage devotional is a great tool for couples who desire increased intimacy with God and each other.

Paul Johnson
CBMC Director of Leader Advancement

***

Wow! This book by John and Sandra Posey is a must-read! This remarkable devotional tool is fully designed to give couples a path to deepen their love for each other. And it will impact your marriage greatly. My wife (Ginger) and I are married for almost 40 years, and we both found the book to be such a need during these times. We highly recommend that you and your spouse use this 52-week devotional to take your marriage to the next level, to become the marriage that God designed it to be. You will be truly blessed.

Mark and Ginger Whitacre
COO, CBMC, Inc.

***

Marriage is full of joys and trials. The Poseys provide sound advice based on their experience and the Word of God. This devotional provides practical application of Biblical principles to address issues which arise in marriage. As married couples, our challenge is to persevere in love and until death do us part.

Dr. Clarisa Haugabrook-Hill, OBGYN

***

In life and love, it's the little things that mean a lot. And in the case of the Poseys, these little things to focus on each week will mean a lot, not just to your spouse, but also in all of your relationships. With simplicity and ease, they give us 52 practical Biblically supported things to do that will make a difference that makes a difference.

Richard D Marks, Ph.D., LPC
Founder, Marriage For Life

***

John and Sandra Posey's 52-week marriage devotional is a fresh, interactive must-read for married couples and singles interested in doing marriage right. Reading this book will make you laugh, contemplate and be challenged to glorify God in your union.

J. Calvin and Kimberly Tibbs
Kingdom Dominion Church, Pastors

***

John and Sandra Posey's 52-week devotional covers every week of the year so that your marriage can follow an established, blessed roadmap to continued love and matrimony.

Minister Floyd and Rev. Gwendolyn Bryant
Floyd & Gwendolyn Foundation

***

John and Sandra Posey have put together in this 52-week marriage devotional a fantastic picture and process of marriage from God's perspective. This 52-week marriage devotional will change your life and your marriage if you will apply the practical steps they outline. Thank you, John and Sandra, for your hearts, your marriage, and your ministry. They are great encouragement and examples to each of us.

Bruce Witt
President, Leadership Revolution

***

Clearly inspired by the Holy Spirit, John and Sandra have composed a beautiful 52-week devotional for married couples.

With wisdom gained through 39 years of marriage, the book is filled with personal stories and supporting scripture as well as tools and practical application of Kingdom principles for marriage.

Indeed, any couple—from newlyweds to empty-nesters—will be inspired and equipped to live out a more abundant and intimate marriage through this beautifully crafted devotional.

Kevin Latty
Executive Director, Souly Business

***

John and Sandra Posey's 52-week *Marriage Equity Devotional* has the Biblical, straight to the point insights you need to help you engage your spouse in godly, practical ways! If you want a street-level view of Biblical marriage and how to grow through your mistakes, this devotional is for you. Get serious, get practical and get *Marriage Equity*!"

Johnny Walker
President, IntegrityATL

***

In *Marriage Equity's 52-Week Devotional: "Invest in Love for a Lifetime Return,"* John and Sandra poignantly share their story of both trial and triumph in ways that resonate deeply. With the thrill and adventure you'd experience on a roller-coaster ride, the reader is quickly captivated and whisked away through the ups and downs of their story, all the while finding hope for their own.

The Poseys don't just share their story; instead, they use it as a springboard for diving into deep areas affecting 21st Century Christian marriages—from money and communication to masturbation and boundaries. Each topic is explored in a simple, bite-sized manner with a practical tip, enriching scripture, simple exercise, meaningful affirmation, and powerful prayer. If you're looking to invest in love for a lifetime return on your marriage, your search is over—this is it!

Dr. Don Brawley III
Influencers Global, President
Canaan Land Church Int'l, Lead Pastor

Dedications

To my Mother, Rosalie Fields Conley

You showed me through your perseverance as a single mother of seven children to never quit, to be strong, to believe in myself regardless. You taught me how to be a survivor under any and every situation. At the age of 71, I have learned how to persevere. You are and always have been my Superhero. I love you to the moon and back.

Your loving daughter,
Sandra

* * *

To my Mom, Pearline Lovette Posey Jones

Mom went home to be with the Lord on February 8, 2018. The day we finished this manuscript was February 8, 2019. The number eight in the Bible represents new beginnings. Mom, you had a new beginning on February 8, 2018, and Sandra and I consider this book to be a new phase or new beginning of our life and ministry on February 8, 2019.

Mom, I dedicate this book to you, because you decided to carry me full term at a time in your life when your pregnancy was truly inconvenient; but you placed your baby boy on the altar of God. What else was I supposed to do with my life, other than to proclaim the Gospel of your God and my God, of your Jesus and my Jesus? Mom, without you there would be no John and Sandra; you were the reason Sandra came to the Lord—your smile, your Bible and the presence of God on your life.

During a very dark time in her life, Sandra looked for your smiling face every day as you both worked in the hospital as nurses. She had lots of questions about God, and you would bring those questions to me. I gave you the answers, and you would go back to this young woman and give her my answer. Finally, you invited her to hear your baby boy preach. My Sandra received Jesus at that service. As she began to make her way to the altar, my Father God spoke to me in what seemed to be an audible voice in my right ear. He said, as Sandra was coming to the altar, "Take a good look at that girl, she is going to be profitable to your ministry." And what a profit she has been, Mom!

Thank you for teaching me the value of reading and the value of learning! I remember your words: "Never throw a book away!" You also taught me to trust in God's power to lead me in Psalm 23 and to protect me and keep me safe in Psalm 27. If I know anything, I know that my God will lead me and my God will protect me, my family and all that I oversee.

Mom, you taught me how to sing to the Lord and enjoy his presence. I love you, Mom, and I will see you again, but not yet! I must be about my Father's business!

From your Baby Boy,
Jonathan (or, as my name means, "God has given")

To Jesus, Prince of Peace

Lord, we dedicate this book to you and to your cause in the earth. Thank you for coming into our lives individually and coming into our marriage when we were struggling in our pride, strife and anger toward each other. After reading the book by your servant John Allan Lavender, *Your Marriage Needs Three Love Affairs*, we realized you were outside of our marriage covenant and we repented! We invited you in, Jesus, and you came into our marriage! Everything changed from that day. It's been almost 40 years, and we shall forever be grateful for that special day! This book is our way to pay it forward and encourage, equip and empower other couples to live according to your design. Thank you, our Savior. May our friends and growth partners know you in marriage the way we know you. Thank you, loving and peaceful Jesus.

Contents

Marriage Investment Stories

Foreword

The story is told of a man and woman at the marriage altar getting ready to recite their wedding vows. The minister finally got to the part where he said, "If there is anyone who objects to this marriage, please speak now or forever hold your peace." The place was so quiet you could hear a pin drop. Then, all of a sudden, a loud voice rang out in the church, "I object, I object!" The minister looked over and said, "You can't object; you're the groom!"

Unfortunately, there are numerous men and women who wish they had objected at their wedding ceremony, because what they thought would be a dream marriage has turned out to be a nightmare. Disappointment, disillusion, frustration and just plain old regret has taken its toll on millions of marriages. But what's the problem? Why are so many marriages ending in divorce? Why are so many marriages just hanging on until the kids are grown and gone? Why are there countless marriages living unhappily ever after, staying together because of financial reasons or convenience, not necessarily because they have a thriving, loving marriage? I believe the answer to those questions lies in the book you have in your hands right now.

Jonathan and Sandra Posey have put together a marvelous resource for married and engaged couples that is Biblical, practical, fun to read and life-changing! I have known this amazing couple for almost 20 years now. They are just as much in love today as they were when I met them! But they don't just have love for each other. They have much more than that. They have a vibrant relationship with Jesus. They have experience (they've been married for almost 40 years!), and they have the wisdom and knowledge that can take your marriage to another level! I'm so grateful they decided to take the time to develop this resource to help make our marriages better.

You may remember the old Beatles song, "All You Need Is Love." Well, I hate to bust your bubble, but when it comes to having a successful marriage, Jonathan and Sandra will tell you that love alone is not enough. Five out of ten marriages today are ending in divorce. Just being in love is simply not enough to sustain a marriage over the long haul. Yes, love is vital, but if you only have love, and you don't possess the tools you need to make your marriage work, then, unfortunately, your marriage, like so many others, won't last. What you need is knowledge, understanding, good counsel, encouragement, extraordinary coaching and practical and Biblical truths. All of that with love is a recipe for an extraordinary marriage!

That's why this 52-week marriage devotional by Jonathan and Sandra Posey is so vital. It is based on God's Word. It is easy to understand. It is hard-hitting. It is relevant. And, it is not overly spiritual. Too many marriage resources deal with esoteric issues rather than the simple fundamentals. People need a resource they can learn to apply to their everyday lives. Jonathan and Sandra have finally created such a resource.

I highly recommend this devotional to anyone who cares about marriage. Even if you're not married, read it. It can prepare you for marriage, or you can use it to bless someone you know.

Marriage is a wonderful thing, but it ain't easy. The first institution God created on the earth was marriage. No wonder marriage it is the institution that is most under attack by the enemy. How do you fight the enemies of divorce and an unfulfilled marriage? It's simple. Read this incredible resource. Read it and grow, like my wife and I did.

Lastly, never forget what marriage is all about. Jonathan and Sandra said it so succinctly and profoundly in this resource: "Marriage is the greatest opportunity of Christ followers to present the Image of God to the world." That's what it's all about, ladies and gentlemen. May God bless your marriage and use it for His glory!

Lee Allen Jenkins
Author, Speaker, Pastor
Eagles Nest Church
Roswell, Georgia

Preface

I (John) was attending Bible school for ministerial training. Each day I had to be at work at one o'clock, and the class would end around noon. I was only ten minutes away from my job, so I took 30 to 45 minutes each day to seek the Lord. One day I was pressing into the presence of God. I was weeping before the Lord and saying, "Lord, I want to finish strong. As I grow older, I want to love and still serve you like I am today. I don't want to be a firecracker preacher, here today and gone tomorrow. So how do I finish strong, how do I complete my assignment?"

I thought the Lord was going to say something profound like "Go to Jerusalem and on the Mount of Olives I will meet you there and do thus and thus!" Instead, the Lord said something so simple yet so profound that I am still feeling the impact of his counsel as when I was 25 years old. The Holy Spirit said, "Master the love walk." In other words, let the love of God, not fortune or fame, be the major pursuit of your life.

My first assignment was to love my Sandra. So I spent a lot time in the Word learning about the love of God. Discovering how to walk in his love toward my Sandra has matured me more than anything. *Agape* love is the most powerful force on earth. When you allow *agape* love to work in your heart, you will never fail. It is this love that is the foundation of our relationship all these years. We say it this way. How you love each other is the DNA of all relationships you will ever have. No other relationship on earth will build character and cultivate *agape* love in your heart like marriage does. This book is about how to deepen your love for one another, through the renewing of your mind by the Word of God and fellowship with God the Holy Spirit. When you activate the Word and the Spirit in your marriage, you will grow deeper in the Lord and overflow into a rich, strife-free, peaceful and satisfying relationship with each other. Take your time with this book and be sure to do the exercises. We can assure you the information between these pages is not something that *might* work. Nor is it just an experiment. These are proven principles that we have used over the last 40 years. They work! May the Lord bless your union!

Introduction

Marriage is the greatest opportunity for Christ followers to present the Image of God to the world. *"Then God said, 'Let us make man in* ***our image, after our likeness****.'" (Genesis 1:26a ESV, emphasis added)* Through a Christ-centered marriage we present a image of love, an image of unity, an image of family, an image of dominion, an image of co-equality, an image of total peace, an image of the celebration of gifts and abilities, an image of submission to one another, an image of roles and functions, an image of teamwork. This list is endless because God is endless.

At the beginning of our marriage, we did not know what a God-designed marriage looked like. We both came from divorced homes. We had no examples of how this marriage thing worked. "You can only live out the pictures you embrace." We want you to think about that statement. Images are very powerful; they shape your beliefs, your values, your expectations. They instill hope or fear. They speak to failure or success.

So, if you have never seen a God-designed marriage, how are you supposed to live it out? God spoke to Moses about building the tabernacle – *"For when Moses was about to erect the tabernacle, he was warned by God, saying, See to it that you make it all [exactly] according to the copy (the model) which was shown to you on the mountain." (Hebrews 8:5b AMPC)* Moses could not build something without SEEING what it looked like. So, we struggled the first few years trying to figure out how to build the thing called marriage.

Once we had "anointed discussions" every day, especially to and from the church. We would get worked up over an issue on the way to church and then press the pause button on the "anointed discussion session," go into the house the Lord and worship him, praise him and listen to his Word from our pastor, fellowship with the saints with hugs and kisses, and leave the service. Then, back in the car on the way home, we'd press the resume button to pick up where we left off!

Well, this went on for a few months until I (John) said to myself, this has to stop! So I was reading in the Bible where it said, *"Wives, be subject (be submissive and adapt yourselves) to your own husbands as [a service] to the Lord. For the husband is head of the wife as Christ is the Head of the church, Himself the Savior of [His] body. As the church is subject to Christ, so let wives also be subject in everything to their husbands."* Of course, I skipped verse 21 – *"Be subject to one another out of reverence for Christ (the Messiah, the Anointed One)."* And I did not see verse 25 – *"Husbands, love your wives, as Christ loved the church and gave Himself up for her" (Ephesians 5:25 AMPC)* The Bible is not a "weapon" for us to use on each other but a rod that we should use on ourselves. Anyway! So, I said to my 20-year-old self (not too smart), "Oh! I see the problem! That woman is in disobedience to the scriptures! I am going to straighten her out!"

So, I couldn't wait for the opportunity to let her know

what she needed to start doing. I walked up to Sandra with the Holy Bible in my hands waving it back and forth (I don't believe I did this!) I raised my voice and said, "Woman, the Bible says you need to submit to me; you need to obey me! Our problems would cease if you just did what the Bible said!" Sandra glared at me with her big beautiful eyes. She snatched the Bible out of my hand, and she hit me in the head with my Holy Bible! She said, "This is what I think about your Bible!" I thought to myself, that's not how I saw that playing out! Just like a boxer once said, "That was my HARDEST punch!" (against the enemy of strife). I had nothing left!

A few weeks later I was shopping at Kroger (this was in 1980). I noticed a book entitled *Your Marriage Needs Three Love Affairs*. "Swinging" had been around about a decade, so I thought it was a book about having open relationships. I thought, what in the world is this godless world talking about now. I picked it up out of curiosity (could be sermon material). This book turned out to be a Christian book, encouraging couples to have a love affair with Jesus individually and then invite Jesus into their marriage as the "third love affair." I read a little bit out of the book, and I realized I had not invited Christ into our relationship even though I was a Christian.

I bought the book and laid it on our kitchen table, hoping Sandra would see it when she got home from work. As she walked through the door and into the kitchen, I looked down at the table to make sure she saw the book. Then she blurted out, "Hey I don't want to have an affair—what are you thinking about!"

I said, "No, no, that's not what this book is about." So we sat down together and began to read that little book. This book changed our trajectory. We were headed for more strife and division, but we made a course correction in our relationship. Following the principles in this book, we "invited" Jesus into our marriage covenant. When Jesus came in, things began to change—not all at once, but little by little. The Holy Spirit began to teach us how to treat each other. We began to grow until we grew out of strife. It took a few years, but by God's grace, we have lived a "strife free" marriage for many, many years.

The takeaways from this story are (1) God will lead you into the kind of connections he wants you to have. We believe the Lord has led us to write this devotional, and we also believe that God has led you to read it! We are connected! There will also be other opportunities beyond this book to make deeper connections. (2) When you are going in the wrong direction, God will apply a course correction. If you will "humble yourself under his mighty hand," he will exalt your marriage to another level. (3) Nothing is permanent in your marriage; you can grow up and grow out of anything! And (4) You don't have to know anything, as long as you are willing to learn "together." Nothing can stop you when you agree about personal growth and development. We chose to grow together for the rest of our lives. We took courses, read books, attended events and did exercises "together." Remember the acrostic for TEAM: Together Everyone Achieves More. We have achieved more together than we had ever thought possible. It's been good!

* * *

We wrote this devotional to give you something to work on consistently. It could be weekly, or the Lord may lead you to stay on a topic until you see the desired results. Be led by the Spirit as you dig into this tool. Also, don't feel you have to follow this book chronologically. You may look through the list of topics and decide on one that is more relevant for you now. So, follow your heart and grow together.

May we pray for you?

Father God, we come to you in the name of Jesus. The name that is above every name. Above the name of divorce, of strife, of irreconcilable differences, pride, abuse, fear, selfishness, indifference, unforgiveness, hopelessness, discouragement, immaturity, harsh communication, sexual dysfunction, emotional disorders, division, hardness of heart, infidelity, substance abuse, and every other name and every demonic force that would rear its ugly head against this most sacred union. Lord God, breathe upon this couple and make yourself known as *Jehovah Shalom*, prince of peace, the Shepherd who will lead this precious couple into green pastures and quiet streams. God Most High, release your healing anointing, and let your rivers of living waters flow from your very throne into this marriage today and this season. We declare, Abba Father, as Obed Edom experienced the ark of God in his home, may the ark of God (the presence of God) fill this marriage and this home right now, most gracious and compassionate Master! By faith, we call it done today. Thank you, precious Holy Spirit. In Jesus' name, we pray! Amen and amen!

The Beginning: Our Story

When I (John) was a baby, my mother caught the bus up to the church and placed me on the altar and asked God to watch after me and protect me, because she was going to have to work 16 hours per day to get her six children out of the projects and off of government assistance. I was never in any trouble in school, and I received Jesus at 15. I accepted the call to preach at 16. I had never smoked a cigarette, done drugs nor was I sexually active. So in Mom's eyes, I was a holy and righteous preacher. She was so proud of me, and I brought my mom great joy. I was completely obedient to her and always showed her honor and respect. To her, I was a perfect child. Of course I was not perfect, but she is a mom!

Mama really liked Sandra; she thought she would be a good wife for one of her sons, just not for her pure baby boy preacher! At the time, I was almost nineteen, and she was twenty-nine. She had a three-year-old child out of wedlock too. Yes, she was a nice girl but not "preacher's wife material." I was not dating at the time because I could not find a girl that loved Jesus as I did. I was already praying for my wife. I had a pretty long list of requirements, I recall. The Lord told me he didn't have anyone like that, but he was going to give me a person with the raw talent to be like that, and I could develop her myself! So here comes beautiful Sandra, a newly saved bouncing baby Christian. The pastor asked me to disciple her, which is really kind of weird when you think about it. (It must have been the Lord.) Sandra was so hungry for God; she would chase me down and asked me to teach her the Bible.

I didn't know much, but I would give her reading assignments, thinking she probably wouldn't do them. Most the people I knew would not follow through at all, but Sandra would come back and say, "I did what you told me to do, what's next?" I began to realize I was going to have to teach this girl the Bible. I started studying a lot more so I could prepare for our sessions. In those early years, she really had no interest in me. I thought she was really a beautiful woman, but I thought she was too old. So, I did not think of her romantically. Our relationship was about growing in Jesus.

I did not realize it at the time, but the Lord was answering my prayer. He said she would be profitable to my ministry, but he did not say this is your wife! If he had told me that, I probably would have freaked out. Sandra saw me as her mentor, and I saw her as my disciple. We began to do things together. I would take her out with me to win souls, and she would help me preach the gospel. That was really cool. She was bold and unashamed of Jesus. I started to like her a little, but I still thought no, she is nice but too old.

We started hanging out together and having fun. Those days, I was about the mission (still like that). What is the next soul to reach, what is the next thing God wants me to do? I didn't have time to play, I had to be about my Father's business. But Sandra would help me take a break and enjoy my life, smell the flowers. So I did, and it was fun to work for Jesus and rest from time to time. (I don't know what I would do without her, she helps me still.)

So one spring day in 1978 we were eating at White Castle, and we started talking about what kind of person we were looking for to date. I began to share what kind of a girl I was looking for. Then she begin to share what kind of a guy she would date. Then all of a sudden, we realized that she was the person I was describing and I was the person she was describing. We stopped and looked at each other. You could tell we had an Aha! moment. (I imagine God was looking at us and saying, "Hello, dudes! I am working on something here!") We became very embarrassed and we both put our heads down and finished our burgers and fries as fast as we could so we could get out of there! That was funny!

After that meal, things began to change. We began to have feelings for each other. But I had a problem; she was too old. I was not a man yet; how could I date an older woman? So I sat down to talk with my oldest sister, Sheila. She was like my second mom. So I would talk to her from time to time about really serious stuff. I would say, "I really like Sandy, but she is too old."

"Yes," Sheila would reply, "She is older than you, but you a very old for your age, and you are going to need an older woman who already has figured some things out. God has called you, Johnny, and you don't have time to waste with a little girl your age; you need a woman. She is perfect for you. I can tell Sandy is helping you to live a little and enjoy your life. You are very happy when you are with her. So it's okay." That's all I needed to hear!

So, I asked Sandra if she would be my girl. She said, "Well, let's just take our time and see what happens." That sounded like a yes to me! I started calling her my girlfriend. I remember our first kiss in her car. She was dropping me off, and I leaned over to kiss her! I ran into the house feeling pretty good! After that kiss, I really open up my heart, and I realized she was the woman I was praying for. After two weeks I was talking on the phone with Sandra during her break at work (she was a surgical technician). During our conversation I said, I love you, Sandy, would you be my wife?" She said yes! We decided to get married in 30 days. (I was really thinking that's about how long I could hold out! Sex in thirty days! Yes!)

Later that week we sat down together with my mom. "Mom," I said, "we are getting married."

"What! You are not out of college yet; you are still living with me, you don't know how to take care of yourself, how will you be able to take care of a wife? Are you pregnant, Sandy?"

"Mom! We are not having sex, that would be a sin against the Lord!"

"Son, you don't have a job, you are not ready for marriage." Mom was right about that, so we got engaged without a wedding date.

In May of 1979, I graduated from the University of Cincinnati with an Electrical Engineering Degree. I started interviewing and got a job offer as a computer technician with Digital Equipment Corporation. I was to start working on Nov 22, 1979. Now that I had a nice job and a good salary, I could take care of myself and my family. We set the wedding date 30 days from my job offer. December 22, 1979 was a year and a half after we had first talked to my mom. That year and a half was really rough because Mom tried her best to convince me not to marry Sandra. She wasn't good enough; she had a past; she would not make a good wife; she wouldn't be able to relate to my friends because of her age; she would look really old as I got older; the list went on and on.

Then Mom started turning our family and church and all of her friends against Sandra. Sandra would cry a lot. On top of the problems on my side, Sandra's family threatened that if she married that preacher, they would disown her. So it was a tough year and a half. One time Mom was really going on about Sandra and how she was really bad for me. I said, "Mom, I love you and I really respect you. You are my mom, but I am going to marry Sandra whether you like it or not. I am telling you, if you don't stop bad-mouthing her with everybody and turning everyone against her, you are going to lose your son. I swear, Mom, I am not going to see you. Sandra will be my wife, and God's Word says to leave your mother and father and cleave to your wife. Don't make me do this, Mom, but I will. I swear!"

Mom never changed her position, and it was very painful to Sandra and me. She did not acknowledge Sandra as a good wife until 25 years later! I understand Mom's struggle, but God was directing me, and I was going to follow the Lord no matter the cost. Mom just could not get past the fact that she was an older woman marrying her baby. She really believed that Sandra was going to wreck my life and that I would also lose the anointing! It is wise to listen to counsel, but at the end of the day, you have to live your own life and follow the Lord.

The only other person who really understood what God was doing was my sister Jackie. Jackie was the reason I received Jesus. She asked me a simple question. I remember we were in the basement of the Finley Street neighborhood house in Cincinnati. We practiced martial arts together. Jackie asked me, "Johnny, I just want to know one thing. I don't care what Mama or anybody else is saying about Sandy. Is God leading you to marry her or not?"

I looked straight into Jackie's eyes and I said, "Jackie, I know in my heart that this marriage is of God."

"That's all I need to hear," she said. "You have my support, my brother." God did lead us, and God did call us together. The struggle was necessary for hard years ahead of us. We learned to stand, pray and fight together. Today we can share our story with you. May the Lord use us to minister to you through this devotional. May the living God build your story for the expansion of his Kingdom!

DEVOTIONALS

Week 1

Keep the air free and the bed hot

If you are angry, there ain't going to be no booty! In other words, if you are constantly in strife, sex is the last thing on your mind.

Tip

Pray for a peaceful relationship. Address one issue at a time and forgive constantly.

Sex should be free, frequent and enjoyable. Sex cultivates true intimacy which is beyond the physical.

We gain knowledge of one another.

Scripture

Let marriage be held in honor among all, and let the marriage bed be undefiled, for God will judge the sexually immoral and adulterous. (Hebrews 13:4 ESV)

For wherever there is jealousy (envy) and contention (rivalry and selfish ambition), there will also be confusion (unrest, disharmony, rebellion) and all sorts of evil and vile practices. (James 3:16 AMPC)

Exercise

Say something encouraging to one another at least once per day.

Block out time for sexual intimacy and be creative.

Affirmation

Today we declare the peace of God, which passes all understanding, in our relationship. We enjoy our time together and purpose to walk in a strife-free marriage. Sex is hot, holy and frequent. Thank you, Jesus.

Prayer

Father God, thank you that we honor our marriage bed and keep it undefiled, holy and hot regularly. We are free from contention, confusion and disharmony. Your peace fills our marriage and overflows into our home.

Week 2

Listen well

God gave you two ears and one mouth, you should be listening twice as much as you are talking.

Tip

Practice active listening by repeating back what your spouse is saying, fully understanding them. Respond only to that issue without defending yourself to prove you are right.

Scripture

Know this, my beloved brothers: let every person be quick to hear, slow to speak, slow to anger. (James 1:19 ESV)

Exercise

In a spirit of humility seek to understand how your spouse feels about what they are sharing.

Put your tongue between your teeth while you are doing this. This way you can't talk. Stay calm and resist anger as you listen. Respond in love.

Affirmation

In the name of Jesus, we empathize with one another's concerns and burdens. We seek to understand before we seek to be understood. We do this in a spirit of Christ-like humility. We will listen wholeheartedly more than we speak. When we speak, it will be with the "God kind" of understanding and wisdom.

Prayer

Father God, thank you that we are active listeners. Help us to walk in the spirit of humility as we seek to understand how we feel as we share our concerns and current pains. In your strength we are quick to hear, slow to speak and slow to become angry. We pull down hurtful, negative and damaging words spoken over each other, and we release words of love, power and encouragement over each other. In the name of Jesus we pray.

Week 3

Still look good!

Your spouse likes to have something to look at.

Tip

After a few years, we can take each other for granted and become so familiar that we don't care about being attractive anymore. Here is the deal: every day your spouse sees attractive people and would like to see the person they love still look good. We get fat, we wear ANYTHING at home, and now we come out of the house *looking* like ANYTHING. We may not brush our teeth, fix our appearance—we just don't care anymore. Still wearing high school size clothes? Come on now! Don't think your spouse doesn't care what you look like. ("Honey, I just love you for you.")

Well, first you should love yourself—like our Mama Pearline always said, "Be particular about yourself"—but you need to also respect your spouse enough to ALWAYS give them something to look at. Don't be fooled, it is still important. So take care of yourself. You both need to be sharp and sexy for your honey.

Scripture

Young Man:

Behold, you are beautiful, my love,

behold, you are beautiful!
Your eyes are doves
behind your veil.
Your hair is like a flock of goats
leaping down the slopes of Gilead.
Your teeth are like a flock of shorn ewes
that have come up from the washing,
all of which bear twins,
and not one among them has lost its young.
Your lips are like a scarlet thread,
and your mouth is lovely.
Your cheeks are like halves of a pomegranate
behind your veil.
Your neck is like the tower of David,
built in rows of stone;
on it hang a thousand shields,
all of them shields of warriors.
Your two breasts are like two fawns,
twins of a gazelle,
that graze among the lilies.
(Song of Solomon 4:1-5 ESV)

Young Woman:
My lover is dark and dazzling,
better than ten thousand others!
His head is finest gold,
his wavy hair is black as a raven.
His eyes sparkle like doves
beside springs of water;
they are set like jewels

washed in milk.
His cheeks are like gardens of spices
giving off fragrance.
His lips are like lilies,
perfumed with myrrh.
His arms are like rounded bars of gold,
set with beryl.
His body is like bright ivory,
glowing with lapis lazuli.
His legs are like marble pillars
set in sockets of finest gold.
His posture is stately,
like the noble cedars of Lebanon.
His mouth is sweetness itself;
he is desirable in every way.
Such, O women of Jerusalem,
is my lover, my friend.

(Song of Solomon 5:10-16 NLT)

Exercise

Make a conscious effort to fix yourself up for your spouse at all times. Look in the mirror after you brush your teeth; put on some attractive clothing that makes you look good. We still need to look attractive to our spouse. Ladies, comb your hair, apply some makeup. Men, shower regularly and put on some nice clothing—underwear included.

Affirmation

We value and care about our spouse enough to look

our best—especially at home when no one else can see us. We will be dazzling and sexy for each other.

Prayer

Father, I thank you that our love and passion for each other increases more and more each day. We beautify ourselves through bathing, clothing, use of make-up (her), perfumes, facial products and anything that will help make us look more attractive to one another. We will not use excuses of any kind that will prevent us from practicing looking good for each other. Father, I will not take for granted my spouse's love and therefore do everything I can to be attractive for him/her. We love each other, and we will do what is necessary to help each other maintain a healthy weight/size that will last the course of our lifetime. When we are old and in our later years, we will be running after each other looking hot and stimulating. Thank you, Father, for keeping us looking hot, sexy and handsome every day of our lives.

Behold, you are beautiful, my love, behold, you are beautiful! (Song of Solomon 4:1 ESV)

Week 4

Cool head, cool money

Strife dries up your money more than anything we have ever seen!

Tip

When you enter into strife, you grieve the Holy Spirit of God who lives within you. You cannot grieve him and have his blessing at the same time. It doesn't work that way. When you are in strife, you cannot hear the still small voice of the Spirit. Why? Because you are making too much noise! Your emotions are out of control, so you cannot make good decisions about anything, including money. Also, the enemy has a legal right to penetrate the hedge of protection around you and yours, because you are breaking the law of love. So, keep a cool head and your money will be "straight"!

Scripture

Likewise, husbands, live with your wives in an understanding way, showing honor to the woman as the weaker vessel, since they are heirs with you of the grace of life, so that your prayers may not be hindered. (1 Peter 3:7 ESV)

Exercise

Stop, listen and be calm when facing conflict. Ask the

Holy Spirit to assist you in a peaceful resolution. Affirm your love for each other, and hug and kiss it out.

Affirmation

Our prayers and connection to God are not hindered; therefore we have an abundance of provision and income because we resolve the conflict by the help of the Holy Spirit.

Prayer

Father God, we thank you that the love we have for each other is stronger than the works of the flesh. We are committed to walking in the love of God and increasingly staying calm when facing conflict. We ask the Holy Spirit to assist us daily to make peaceful resolutions that will bring us closer together. We will not allow strife and anger to hinder our love and ability to prosper. We affirm each other, being mindful of our deep love for each other, and we hug and kiss it out at all times.

Week 5

Communication, part 1

Miscommunication is the number one reason for divorce. Love-filled communication is a must. We must stay free from negative, hateful words that undermine and destroy our relationship.

Tip

Refuse to place blame on each other and fight over issues A, B and C. Take on one issue at a time in the peace of God, being mindful that your spouse is a part of the body of Christ. Therefore, what you do to them you do to Jesus. The Holy Spirit in you is taking note of your behavior. So, keep your mouth free from foul and polluted language.

Scripture

Let no foul or polluting language, nor evil word nor unwholesome or worthless talk [ever] come out of your mouth, but only such [speech] as is good and beneficial to the spiritual progress of others, as is fitting to the need and the occasion, that it may be a blessing and give grace (God's favor) to those who hear it. (Ephesians 4:29 AMPC)

Exercise

Practice self-control, be slow to speak and quick to hear. Speak three admirable positive traits to each other daily.

Affirmation

We will not let foul or polluting language nor any evil word nor unwholesome or worthless talk to ever come out of our mouth, but we will only use such speech as is good and beneficial to the spiritual progress of our sweetheart—powerful faith-filled words as is fitting to the need and the occasion, that it may be a blessing and give grace (God's favor) to my love.

Prayer

Father God, in the name of Jesus as husband and wife, we will not let any foul polluting language nor evil word nor unwholesome or worthless talk to ever come out of our mouth. We are deeply in love with each other and we cherish each other with reverence and respect, knowing that unwholesome words destroy and undermine us as individuals. So our speech is good and beneficial to the spiritual progress of one another. We speak words that are fitting to each other so that they may be a blessing and give grace (God's favor) to us.

A Marriage Investment Story . . .

The car

It was 1986. Sandra and I were working on saving money. After a lot of hard work, we finally saved $1,000. We were pretty excited about that. I decided to stop by a car lot and check out a few cars. The salesman came out and began to show me the new Hyundai. The price of the car was about $5,500. I had good credit, and I made enough money. I just needed $1,000 as a down payment.

So, since I had the money, I emptied our savings account and got my new car! I was excited about it. The only problem is I did not consult Sandra about it. I just felt I had the right to get whatever I wanted. I am the man, and that's it! So, I came home to show her the car and take her for a ride. She asked, "Where did you get this car!"

"I bought it today at the car lot. It cost $5,500, and I had good credit. I just needed $1,000 down, so I bought it."

"What $1,000 are you talking about?"

"The $1,000 in our savings account."

"You spent all of our money!"

"Yes, I did."

"You did not ask me about it?"

"No, I didn't."

"Why did you think you could do this without talking to me?"

"Because I can!"

"I will never trust you again!"

She really got mad. I honestly did not realize that I needed to ask her anything. I was making the income, so subconsciously I did not think she had any rights. It's my money so that is that! But that is not true. She is doing the most important job for our family—raising our children and creating an environment for us to live a peaceful life. She has every right to any and everything we have. We are a team. She is playing a different position, but it is not less important than mine. She certainly was capable of working outside the home with her skills. But she made a choice to raise our children. She felt it was important for this season of our lives. And she was right. Sandra seemed to always know what was right for our family, and she was always in touch with what we needed. I was checked out most of the time working on my mission, but she always kept me grounded.

Well, this car later proved to have a host of problems—transmission, engine. (I believe it was cursed, because of my arrogance.) I hired a guy to replace my engine. So, he put my car on the side of the house and took my money and left my car on bricks and never fixed the half-torn-apart engine! I refinanced the car two times due to some financial challenges. I ended up paying three times as much as the car was worth, and when I finally got the title, the car was broken down on the side of our house. I was so mad I threw the title at the car!

Well, I learned the hard way to listen to my wife and include her on all decisions. Sandra is really smart and after a 39-year track record, she has never been wrong about anything! I mean anything—in a business deal, about any person or any situation. If Sandra says something is wrong about it, something is wrong about it! I had better listen! I learned through this situation (and unfortunately a few other incidents) to listen to my wife. She is my greatest asset. I call her my secret weapon!

Week 6

Communication, part 2

Miscommunication is the number one reason for divorce. When you win in a communication exchange, everybody loses.

Tip

Avoid a prideful, contentious "I want to win this verbal war" mindset. Nothing but evil and destruction will come out of such a carnal attitude.

Scripture

For you are still [unspiritual, having the nature] of the flesh [under the control of ordinary impulses]. For as long as [there are] envying and jealousy and wrangling and factions among you, are you not unspiritual and of the flesh, behaving yourselves after a human standard and like mere (unchanged) men? (1 Corinthians 3:3 AMPC)

For wherever there is jealousy (envy) and contention (rivalry and selfish ambition), there will also be confusion (unrest, disharmony, rebellion) and all sorts of evil and vile practices. (James 3:16 AMPC)

Exercise

When communicating with each other, take a moment to pause and "seek to understand instead of seeking to be understood." The goal is resolution, which requires compromise and yielding to one another. More importantly, that involves yielding and submitting to the Word of God regarding "love your neighbor as yourself." How would you want your spouse to treat you? Be first!

Affirmation

We declare that we will completely avoid prideful and arrogant communications with each other that undermine the foundation of our love for each other. We bind up the "I want to win this verbal war" mindset in our marriage. We will not allow carnal and critical words and attitudes to destroy our marriage through carnal outbursts.

Prayer

Father, thank you for your wisdom that daily flows down from your throne into our marriage. We submit our thoughts, words and attitudes to the Word of God. We dedicate ourselves to live a strife-free marriage, never seeking an "I will win this verbal war" mindset. Father, cleanse us with the power of your Word so that we will not sin against you. We will not be controlled by ordinary impulses and strife triggers from past issues. We bind up jealousy and envying spirits of discord, which would love to penetrate our marriage and bring it to destruction. Father, pour out the power of your Holy Spirit on us today, and strengthen us to be a couple who walks with God, overcoming the power of evil-speaking in our marriage.

We will not fall into the trap of winning an argument, because when you win in a communication exchange, everybody loses. Thank you, Father, that we are winning because we walk in love with each other.

Week 7

Sex, part 1

Overcome hindrances to a healthy sexual life.

Tip

Reset your sexual purity through forgiving yourself of unbiblical relationships.

Scripture

How much more will the blood of Christ, who through the eternal Spirit offered himself without blemish to God, purify our conscience from dead works to serve the living God. (Hebrews 9:14 ESV)

Exercise

Have personal communion with your spouse. When you take communion, say this. This broken body of Jesus (bread), represents God's healing power to my past sexual life. Because Jesus' body is pure, my body is now pure. I take the cup (grape juice) for the complete forgiveness of my sins. I no longer have a conscience of guilt and condemnation. I am clean through the blood of Christ, and I am free to have holy, pure sex with my love.

Affirmation

Because we are cleansed through the body and blood

of Jesus Christ, we are cleansed and free from past unbiblical sexual relationships. The blood and body of Jesus have made us free from guilt and condemnation. We are now able to have healthy, clean sexual relationships with each other and be fully satisfied.

Prayer

Father God, thank you for freedom through the blood of Jesus. We are free to love and fulfill each other's sexual desires without feeling unclean and guilty. We embrace each other intimately and bask in each other's presence while fully enjoying the freedom that comes from your healing. Thank you, Father God, that we will continuously love each other passionately without hindrances of the past. We do not allow negative thoughts to come and steal our freedom. In the name of Jesus, we bind up the lying tongues of demons and harassing spirits from coming to steal this wonderful freedom we have from you. We only allow our thoughts to be filled with love for each other as we freely give ourselves to one another.

Week 8

Sex, part 2

While adultery is no longer a deal breaker in many marriages, infidelity is one of the top-cited reasons couples decide to get divorced.

The experts at *Divorce Magazine* note that about 45-50 percent of married women and 50-60 percent of married men cheat on their spouses.

When couples stop having sex, their relationships become vulnerable to anger, detachment, infidelity and, ultimately, divorce.

Tip

Have sex as a priority in your marriage. Work on this area of your relationship as if your marriage depended on it.

Scripture

Now, getting down to the questions you asked in your letter to me. First, Is it a good thing to have sexual relations? Certainly—but only within a certain context. It's good for a man to have a wife, and for a woman to have a husband. Sexual drives are strong, but marriage is strong enough to contain them and provide for a balanced and fulfilling sexual life in a world of sexual disorder. The marriage bed must be a place of mutuality—the husband seeking to satisfy his wife, the wife seeking to satisfy her husband. Marriage is not a place to "stand up for your rights." Marriage is a decision to serve the other, whether in bed or out. Abstaining from sex is permissible for a period of time if you both agree to it, and if it's for the purposes of prayer and fasting—but only for such times. Then come back together again. Satan has an ingenious way of tempting us when we least expect it. (1 Corinthians 7:2-6 The Message)

Exercise

Rate your sexual satisfaction on a scale of one ten. One being extremely dissatisfied and ten being extremely satisfied. Ask your spouse what "extremely satisfied" looks like to them. Please be specific. Note: stay positive, without judgment, and seek help if required.

Affirmation

It's good for a man to have a wife, and a woman to have a husband. Our sexual drives are very strong toward each other. We decree that we consistently strive towards sexual fulfillment with each other. Our marriage bed is a place of agreement; we seek to extremely satisfy each other sexually. We declare our marriage is a place to love, serve and satisfy each other. The Lord has healed us from sexual hang-ups and hindrances from the past. We agree that abstaining from sex is permissible for a period of time if we both agree to it and if it's for the purposes of prayer and fasting—but only for such times. Then we will come back together again. We declare we will not allow Satan to tempt us in any way when we least expect it.

Prayer

Father God, we thank you for bringing healing and health to our marriage bed. Our marriage bed is consistently filled with deep passion for love and freedom. On a scale of one to ten we never fail to receive a ten from each other. Father, help us to keep the passion and fire burning in our intimacy with each other. We are seeking to always bring the very best of our love to our bedroom regularly. We abstain only in times of seeking you, but afterward we quickly return to sharing our love for each other. Thank you, Father, for this gift of expressing our love to each other.

Week 9

Money, part 1

God owns everything, and we get to manage it for him. The responsible management of these God-given resources is called stewardship.

Stewardship in marriage in critical to the health of your overall marriage experience; therefore God must be first in this number two reason for divorce.

Tip

Transfer ownership of your finances over to the Lord, for he is the reason and source of your increase.

Scripture

The earth and everything in it, the world and its inhabitants, belong to the Lord. (Psalm 24:1 ESV)

Riches and honor come from You, and You are the ruler of everything. Power and might are in Your hand, and it is in Your hand to make great and to give strength to all. (1 Chronicles 29:12 ESV)

Every generous act and every perfect gift is from above, coming down from the Father of lights; with Him there is no variation or shadow cast by turning. (James 1:17 ESV)

Whatever you do, do it enthusiastically, as something done for the Lord and not for men, knowing that you will receive the reward of an inheritance from the Lord. You serve the Lord Christ. (Colossians 3:23-24 ESV)

"His master said to him, 'Well done, good and faithful slave! You were faithful over a few things; I will put you in charge of many things. Share your master's joy!'" (Matthew 25:21 ESV)

Precious treasure and oil are in the dwelling of a wise person, but a foolish man consumes them. (Proverbs 21:20 ESV)

Honor the Lord with your possessions and with the first produce of your entire harvest. (Proverbs 3:9 ESV)

For to everyone who has, more will be given, and he will have more than enough. But from the one who does not have, even what he has will be taken away from him. (Matthew 25:29 ESV)

Based on the gift each one has received, use it to serve others, as good managers of the varied grace of God. (1 Peter 4:10 ESV)

So if you have not been faithful with the unrighteous money, who will trust you with what is genuine? (Luke 16:11 ESV)

Remember this: The person who sows sparingly will also reap sparingly, and the person who sows generously will also reap generously. Each person should do as he has decided in his heart—not reluctantly or out of necessity, for God loves a cheerful giver. (2 Corinthians 9:6-7 ESV)

Exercise

Review your overall giving from last year. Review key scriptures regarding stewardship and build your faith on these, trusting God with the resources he has given you to manage.

Affirmation

We will honor God with our first fruits and all our income; then our saving accounts, checking accounts and household will be filled with plenty. We agree as a couple to take our tithes and offerings out first and dedicate them to the Lord. We are managers of the financial resources you have given us; you are the owner. We will obey you by bringing what is yours to your storehouse, the place where you have called us to worship. We will yield to a spirit of generosity and give to ministries and causes that match our passion.

Prayer

Father God, you are the owner of everything. The earth belongs to you, and everything we have is yours, including our money. In fact, it is not our money because everything we have belongs to you and we are the stewards. As stewards, we will manage the resources we have following your Word and obeying the promptings of your Spirit.

Week 10

Money, part 2

Roughly two million marriages take place each year, according to the National Center for Health Statistics. At the same time, there are about 800,000 divorces or annulments. The leading cause of stress in a relationship is finances, according to a 2015 study by SunTrust Bank.

Tip

Discuss your mutual financial goals, write them down and spend one prayer session a week praying over your financial goals.

Scripture

Christ redeemed us from the curse of the law by becoming a curse for us—for it is written, "Cursed is everyone who is hanged on a tree"—so that in Christ Jesus the blessing of Abraham might come to the Gentiles, so that we might receive the promised Spirit through faith. (Galatians 3:13-14 ESV)

Exercise

Create a financial "dream board" and discuss the reason why these goals are important to you as a couple. Spend once a week looking at your financial dream board and visualize yourselves fulfilling your financial goals.

Affirmation

We declare that according to God's Word, Christ redeemed us from the curse of the law [including poverty and lack] by becoming a curse for us—for it is written, "Cursed is everyone who is hanged on a tree"—so that in Christ Jesus the blessing of Abraham might come upon [us]. We are free from lack, poverty and debt in Jesus' name. The Holy Spirit will lead us out of debt into abundance so that we are in a position to be a blessing to God's kingdom and his cause in the earth.

Prayer

Father, thank you for redeeming us from the curse of the law and sending Jesus to become a curse for us. *"For it is written, 'Cursed is everyone who is hanged on a tree'—so that in Christ Jesus the blessing of Abraham might come to the Gentiles, so that we might receive the promised Spirit through faith." (Galatians 3:13-14 ESV)* We are blessed and not cursed in everything we do, and the blessings of our God are upon us every day. Even though over 800,000 divorces or annulments occur each year, divorce will not come near our dwelling. We seek first the kingdom of God and your righteousness.

Week 11

Honoring her

Husbands should understand and be considerate of their wives' spiritual, emotional and physical needs. It is the husband's responsibility to protect and care for his wife, "just as Christ does the church" (Ephesians 5:28-30). Also, husbands are to treat their wives with respect as the weaker partner. "Weaker" (*asthenesterō*) refers to physical or emotional weakness, not intellectual inferiority, for wives are their husbands' fellow heirs of God's gift of life.

Tip

Show your wife honor and respect by opening the door for her, standing when she comes into the room, offering her a seat first—giving her a hug each day without sexual advances. Complement her on some attribute that is not sexual (for example, not "you have great boobs" or "a nice booty"). Tell her how attractive she is to you, especially when she is no longer youthful and has had multiple children, and her body has changed since being a young woman.

Scripture

Likewise, husbands, live with your wives in an understanding way, showing honor to the woman as the weaker vessel, since they are heirs with you of the grace of life, so that your prayers may not be hindered. (1 Peter 3:7 ESV)

Exercise

Pray for your wife this week. Ask her about specific areas she would like you to pray for. Also, say something encouraging and edifying. Be specific and exact with your words. This week, text her something that you know she loves to hear.

Affirmation

I honor, respect and give praises to my wife continuously as I speak sweet words of comfort and support. I scream to the top of my voice, "My wife is the most beautiful woman in the world!" I tell her how much I am attracted to her without any sexual agendas. I tell my wife that just being with her makes me "feel Like Superman." The Lord renews her youth like an eagle; she looks more beautiful and younger as the years go by. I hug her each day without sexual advances. Even after multiple children and many years gone by, my love becomes more beautiful to me.

Prayer

Father God, thank you for making me a loving and understanding husband. Fill me with wisdom to love and honor my sweetheart. I will always protect her and give her deep emotional support. Thank you for showing me how to love her as Christ loves the church. As her husband, I am in tune with her emotional needs and desires. I will constantly show her admiration with sweet, tender words. I will never stop showing her how beautiful she is and how much I love being with her. You said in your Word, whoever finds a wife finds a good thing. Father, I will forever give you praise for bringing me such a gorgeous, attractive and beautiful wife. I will honor my darling and treat her like she is the most wonderful gift to me from my heavenly Father. Thank you, Jesus.

Week 12

Admiration for him

Your man needs admiration like he needs oxygen. It is essential for his emotional health. He needs to feel that you see him as powerful and strong and capable of anything.

Tip

Wives, understand and appreciate your husband more than anyone else. Remind him this week of his value and achievements. Tell him, "Honey, I believe in you." Avoid criticizing him. Let him know you are proud of him, not out of duty, but from a profound respect for the man you chose to marry.

Scripture

The same goes for you wives: Be good wives to your husbands, responsive to their needs. There are husbands who, indifferent as they are to any words about God, will be captivated by your life of holy beauty. What matters is not your outer appearance—the styling of your hair, the jewelry you wear, the cut of your clothes—but your inner disposition.

Cultivate inner beauty, the gentle, gracious kind that God delights in. The holy women of old were beautiful before God that way, and were good, loyal wives to their husbands. Sarah, for instance, taking care of Abraham, would address him as "my dear husband." You'll be true daughters of Sarah if you do the same, unanxious and unintimidated. (1 Peter 3:1-6 The Message)

Exercise

Highlight something your husband has done in the past, some achievement and accomplishment, and let him know how much you admire him for this accomplishment and achievement. When he does something good, pause for a moment and tell him, "That's what I love about you, baby!"

Affirmation

He that finds a wife finds a good thing. I am so thankful for finding my true love. My spouse is a man of honor, integrity and strength. I constantly admire his great qualities, determination and no-quit attitude; failure is not an option. My love always makes me feel like a woman adorned with love and understanding. He is the best thing that God has given to me. I never need to fear what the future will hold. I tell him constantly, "You are the love of my life and I would not want to spend my life with anyone else." God knew what he was doing when he put him in my life. My man is a mighty conqueror, I believe my sweetheart can do everything he puts his hands to. He is my earthly hero. I believe in my man with all of my heart.

Prayer

I worship and adore you, Lord Most High. Pour out your amazing grace on me to walk in love, understanding and appreciation for him. You blessed him with courage, power and love for me. I believe he is the best thing that has ever happened to me. Lord show me how to express my love towards him, so he knows how much I truly respect, love and cherish him. Help me understand and appreciate my husband more than anyone else. Lord, help me to cultivate my inner beauty, which is the gentle, gracious kind that God delights in. I am a good, loyal wife to my husband. I commit each week to remind him of his value and achievements. With your help, Lord, I delight in telling him that I believe in him and he is capable of being successful in all things in life. I believe in my charming knight in shining armor, my gift from God.

A Marriage Investment Story . . .

Spoiled milk

I was in Bible school in 1983 in Tulsa, Oklahoma. I had a job with Digital Equipment Corporation (DEC) as a computer technician. Sandra worked at home raising our children, so money was tight. If we wanted to buy milk, we would have to dig through the car seat sometimes to find a few coins to cover expenses. Rhema Bible Training Center had a strict late policy—if you were late to class so many times, you could get kicked out of school. So I was never late.

Anyway, our refrigerator did not cool well, and the milk tasted a little spoiled, so I poured it down the kitchen sink. Sandra got mad, because we did not have food to waste. I got upset about how she was acting, so I headed out the door, slamming it behind me. (I think I had this thing about slamming doors.) I was spitting mad on the way to Bible school. On my way, God opened my spiritual ears, and I heard the voice of demons saying, "They are in strife, and we are going to have all day to do some damage!" When I heard this, I freaked out, but I thought, "If I turn around, I am going to be late to school. But If I don't get this right, I am putting my family at risk." So I turned around and went back home.

I got on my knees and rang the doorbell. Sandra

came to the door, I said, "Sandra, I am so sorry for acting like that, please forgive me." She turned her head away and walked back in the living room. So I followed her scooting on my knees! I grabbed her around her waist with my head in her bosom. "Please, Sandra, I am sorry." She melted and said okay! We kissed and made up. Ha, ha on the devil! I went on to school that day. Yes, I got a late slip, but I was in the will of God and protected from the enemy by the power of the Holy Spirit. (Psalm 91)

Week 13

Be a house, not a car, part 1

A car loses value when you drive it off the lot. Many couples lose their value after the marriage ceremony because they feel they have their man/woman, so the work is over! "You are mine now, so I don't need to do anything special because I got you!" Divorce is the result of the loss of value of your spouse.

Tip

Never take each other for granted. Make it your aim to seek to please each other and be and look good for each other. Continue to develop your relationship skills. Work on yourself instead of shaping and molding your spouse into the person you want them to be.

Scripture

No one abuses his own body, does he? No, he feeds and pampers it. That's how Christ treats us, the church since we are part of his body. And this is why a man leaves his father and mother and cherishes his wife. No longer two, they become "one flesh." This is a huge mystery, and I don't pretend to understand it all. What is clearest to me is the way Christ treats the church. And this provides a good picture of how each husband is to treat his wife, loving himself in loving her, and how each wife is to honor her husband. (Ephesians 5:29-33 The Message)

Exercise

Review the summary of *His Needs, Her Needs: Building an Affair-Proof Marriage* by Willard Harley using the URL below:

https://joshfowleronline.com/2015/02/15/his-needs-her-needs-10-emotional-needs-in-marriages/

Affirmation

We are not abusive in any way to each other. We treat each other with honor and respect. We are growing up and growing strong together. Our lives are conforming into the image and likeness of Jesus Christ our Lord. We are truly becoming one flesh on a daily basis. We provide a good picture of how each husband is to treat his wife, loving himself in loving her, and how each wife is to honor her husband.

We declare we are a house and not a car. We are delighted to look the best for each other. We never take each other for granted. When the evening comes, we can wrap each other up in our undying love for one another. We aim to please each other to look the best for each other.

Prayer

Father God, thank you for the power of your compassion and love overshadowing us every day. Create in us a deep desire to please each other. We keep our hearts beating strong for each other, never taking each other for granted or doing little to keep ourselves looking good. Father, remove from our hearts the attitude of marriage being a destination instead of a marathon. Remove our selfishness and laziness that would keep us from doing our best to look good and strive to be the best we can be. Thank you, Father, for your steadfast love over our marriage.

Week 14

Be a house, not a car, part 2

Appreciation is an increase in the value of an asset over time. In the same way, your marriage is like a house. Your relationship should increase in its value. Therefore your marriage is adding value to who you are as a person and what you are capable of being. The day you were married was the WORST you would ever be!

Tip

Select a book on marriage and set time aside each week to read it together. Discuss a key point that impacts you and write down key points you can practice immediately. See our book reading list on our website:

www.MarriageEquitySystems.com

Scripture

But the fruit of the Spirit is love, joy, peace, patience, kindness, goodness, faithfulness, gentlenesses, self-control; against such things there is no law. And those who belong to Christ Jesus have crucified the flesh with its passions and desires. If we live by the Spirit, let us also keep in step with the Spirit. Let us not become conceited, provoking one another, envying one another. (Galatians 5:22-26 ESV)

Exercise

Review the verses from 1 Corinthians 13:4-8 below. Highlight areas you need to improve in loving your spouse. Pray and ask the Holy Spirit to help you walk the area you need to improve in. Tell your spouse the area. (Note to spouse: do not say, "Yes, I know, and finally you see your mess!" Rather, listen and support your spouse.) Ask your spouse to hold you accountable to what you desire to improve in.

"Love endures long and is patient and kind; love never is envious nor boils over with jealousy, is not boastful or vain-glorious, does not display itself haughtily.

"It is not conceited (arrogant and inflated with pride); it is not rude (unmannerly) and does not act unbecomingly. Love (God's love in us) does not insist on its own rights or its own way, for it is not self-seeking; it is not touchy or fretful or resentful; it takes no account of the evil done to it [it pays no attention to a suffered wrong].

"It does not rejoice at injustice and unrighteousness, but rejoices when right and truth prevail.

"Love bears up under anything and everything that comes, is ever ready to believe the best of every person, its hopes are fadeless under all circumstances, and it endures everything [without weakening].

"Love never fails [never fades out or becomes obsolete or comes to an end]. As for prophecy (the gift of interpreting the divine will and purpose), it will be fulfilled and pass away; as for tongues, they will be destroyed and cease; as for knowl-

edge, it will pass away [it will lose its value and be superseded by truth]." (1 Corinthians 13:4-8 AMPC)

Affirmation

We understand the power of valuing and showing appreciation to each other. We aggressively make use of resources that will cause us to increase our value to one another. We declare that our marriage is like a house, so we invest time and effort to increase our love and appreciation. We select books and other resources every week to strengthen specific areas in our relationship.

Prayer

Father, your Word says all things work together for good to those who are called according to your purpose. Thank you, Father, for showing us how to bring value to one another. Lead us by your Holy Spirit and teach us how to walk in the fruit of the Spirit. We are committed to walking in love, joy, peace, patience, kindness, goodness, faithfulness and self-control—against such things there is no law. We meditate on scriptures that will increase our love and patience. Father, help us to never condemn and criticize each other's weaknesses.

Week 15

Do you have a plan?

Do you have a plan for your marriage? Ninety percent of all businesses fail within the first two years. The number one reason is undercapitalization; the number two reason is no business plan. We plan our marriage event, but we don't have a plan for our marriage. Now, does that make any sense?

Tip

Use the outline provided on our website to complete the exercise this week and start working on your customized "Happy Marriage Plan."

www.MarriageEquitySystems.com
(See the marriage plan tab.)

Scripture

For which of you, desiring to build a tower, does not first sit down and count the cost, whether he has enough to complete it? Otherwise, when he has laid a foundation and is not able to finish, all who see it begin to mock him, saying, "This man began to build and was not able to finish." (Luke 14:28 ESV)

Exercise

Type up and print out the first phase of your marriage plan. Place it somewhere you can see it this week. Read it out loud and use the prayer below to ask for God's wisdom in building out the rest of your plan.

Affirmation

We secure the success of our marriage by implementing a "Happy Marriage Plan." We use our marriage plan to guide us into developing a strong, fail-proof marriage that will last. Just like a business plan is necessary for business success, we are using our marriage plan to make sure it excels. We desire to build a stronger marriage unit. We sit down and count the cost and so make sure our marriage will go the distance for all the days of our lives.

Prayer

Father, pour out your lovingkindness and tender mercies upon our marriage. We submit our "Happy Marriage Plans" to you, for you said in your Word that we are blessed and not cursed. We surrender our plans to your mighty counsel of wisdom and leadership. Lead us into a successful marriage union that will stand the test of time. Father, without you we can do nothing but make a mess. We ask you to bless, develop and grow our marriage until it is complete with happiness and joy.

Week 16

24 hours

Never allow a break in your fellowship as a couple to go more than twenty-four hours. Don't carry over your disagreement and strife to the next day, or you will experience the power of negative compound interest.

Tip

Resolve your issue quickly, when you can talk about it. Literally kiss and make up. Ask God's forgiveness, each other's forgiveness; hold and pray for each other with humility and love. Ask God's blessing on your union.

Scripture

Be angry and do not sin; do not let the sun go down on your anger, and give no opportunity to the devil. (Ephesians 4:26-27 ESV)

Exercise

If you collide over an issue, stop and repent to God and each other. Seek to understand how your spouse feels about the disagreement and apologize for hurting each other. Then discuss reasonable solutions without judgment and fault-finding. Make it a point to do what you can agree on. Remember to be reasonable and unselfish.

Affirmation

We are a loving and understanding couple, and we do not allow breaks in our fellowship to go beyond 24 hours. We resolve issues quickly. We do not allow disagreements and strife to roll over to the next day and receive the power of negative compound interest. Our love for each other is more important than allowing strife and anger to bring destruction to the continuity of our relationship. When we are angry, we refuse to give Satan a foothold by allowing sin to enter. We always stop and repent to God and each other to resolve issues quickly.

Prayer

Bless the Lord, O my soul, and all that is within me bless his holy name. Thank you, Father, for the wisdom in the 24-hour rule that you give us. We will never allow a break in our fellowship as a couple. Father, strengthen us to respect and honor the 24-hour rule and never allow issues to flow over to the next day, bringing negative compound interest. When we are angry with each other, we will repent and forgive quickly.

Week 17

Forgiveness

"Refusing to forgive someone is like drinking poison and expecting the other person to die." —Bruce Hebel, *Forgiving Forward*

Tip

Forgiveness is the very crux of the Christian faith. It is why Jesus came to earth to die on the cross, to forgive us for our sins (Romans 5:8, 1 John 1:9). In *Forgiving Forward*, Bruce and Toni Hebel point out how critical it is for us to forgive others and to do so quickly. Not only is it necessary for our personal health and well-being, but it is also important for our witness. They say, "Perhaps the most significant reason God takes unforgiveness so seriously is that our witness to the Gospel is compromised when we are not modeling what Jesus did for us." As a couple, unforgiveness can erode the very foundation of your holy union.

Scripture

Be kind to one another, tenderhearted, forgiving one another, as God in Christ forgave you. (Ephesians 4:32 ESV)

Exercise

Examine your words this week. How many of them refer to or bring up past issues? Check your heart for resentment and bitterness. If you need to talk about it with your spouse, do so with an attitude of humility. Talk it over, resolve it and let it go. If you have already talked over issues, make an effort not to bring them up. If they come into your mind, stop and say out loud, "I forgive my spouse for that offense, since God has forgiven me for my sins against him. I am free in my heart today!"

Affirmation

We are filled with the same forgiving heart, mind and attitude of Jesus Christ. We examine our words this week to make sure we do not bring up past issues. We check our heart to make sure we are free from all resentment and bitterness. We observe the 24-hour rule which says, "After 24 hours we must let it go." We keep our hearts free from immature fleshly behavior that Satan tries to use against us to trap us in sin.

Prayer

Father, we are kind to one another, tenderhearted, forgiving one another, as God in Christ forgave us. We humble ourselves under your mighty hand, and you will exalt us in due time. Jesus, you came to the earth to forgive us and die for our sins. Help us to forgive forward and to always observe the 24-hour rule. Thank you, Father, that as a couple we will not allow unforgiveness to erode the very foundation of our love. Father, touch and strengthen us to walk in forgiveness.

Week 18

Strife

Living in a "strife free" environment is possible for the Spirit-filled, Spirit-led Christian.

Tip

Understand that strife opens the door to everything the thief has in his arsenal. It may feel good to "let your spouse have it," especially if you are hurting. But when you yield to strife, it's the same as chewing off your own foot, cutting off your own hand or gouging out your own eyes because you are *one flesh*; doing this to your spouse is doing this to yourself. Strife is a no-win scenario. So decide that strife may come to the door of your marriage, but you don't have to open the door. If just one of you can believe the Word in this area and honor the Spirit of God in you, strife will *never* enter in.

Scripture

For where envying and strife is, there is confusion and every evil work. (James 3:16 KJV)

Exercise

Commit James 3:16 to memory through meditating on this verse before each meal. When you have an opportunity to enter into strife, let James manage your emotions so that you don't chew off your own foot. (Get a picture of a dog chewing off his own foot, then saying to himself, "I won that battle!" Really?) Hurting each other through strife is self-afflicting and self-mutilation, you must see this. Consider Ephesians 5:28-29 – *"In the same way husbands should love their wives as their own bodies. He who loves his wife loves himself. For no one ever hated his own flesh, but nourishes and cherishes it, just as Christ does the church." (ESV)*

Affirmation

We are living in a "strife free" environment with the help of the Holy Spirit, our Helper. We commit to being slow to speak, slow to wrath and quick to hear. We are active listeners, listening to hear the heart of one another and not waiting to be heard. We shut the door to bad-mouthing each other, chewing each other out and holding grudges. Strife is a no-win scenario, so we decide that strife may not come into our marriage. Strife, we speak to you in the name of Jesus, and we say get out of our marriage now!

Prayer

All glory, honor and power belong to you, God of Heaven. You are the possessor of Heaven and Earth. We exalt you and give you praise. Your Word says in James 3:16, *"For where envying and strife is, there is confusion and every evil work." (KJV)* Lord, teach us to be doers of the Word and not hearers only. Strengthen us to resist sinning against you and each other. It is not by might nor by power but by your Spirit that we can overcome strife and every evil thing in our marriage.

A Marriage Investment Story . . .

You don't have to be in the car late at night; I have already done that!

"Be angry and do not sin; do not let the sun go down on your anger." (Ephesians 4:26 ESV)

This happened early in our marriage, when we were still trying to navigate through strife issues. It was 20 degrees F in the early 1980s in Cincinnati. Sandra and I argued about something. I got so mad and decided to go outside late that night. I remember slamming the door when I went outside as hard as I could. You know, I tried to shake the apartment so she could know how pissed I was! I sat in my 1973 Cutlass with a hole in the floor and a bad muffler. I started the car up to stay warm, but the fumes from the muffler came up through the floor. I thought, "If I keep the car running, I will probably die in here!" So, I turned the car off.

As I sat in the very cold car the scripture came to mind, *"Be angry and do not sin; do not let the sun go down on your anger." (Ephesians 4:26 ESV)* No doubt the Holy Spirit was trying to help me. I remember saying, "Yeah, I know that verse, but it says don't go to bed angry. So, I will stay up all night; this way I am not disobeying the Word and I can still be pissed! But that's not what it says! *"Be angry and do not sin;* ***do not let the sun go down*** *on your anger" (Ephesians 4:26 ESV, emphasis added)*, What is it saying here? Resolve your issues, and don't carry them over to the next day, and the next day, and the next day!

It was getting later and later (probably 3:00 in the morning). I was wrapped up in a blanket, shivering! I remembered we had a very nice warm water bed. We bought it so we could have great sex! I begin to think, "Here I am outside in the cold, I will probably freeze to death, and I have a gorgeous woman upstairs in that nice warm water bed! For what? This is really stupid!" So, I sheepishly went back into the house, only to find Sandra asleep! I woke her up and apologized. "I am sorry, Sandra."

Week 19

Completion, not competition

Your spouse can be considered as a threat or as an asset. It all depends on how you think about strengths, abilities and expertise. It all depends on the way you see yourself: Are you a team or two individuals who struggle for value and significance?

Tip

Celebrate each other's talents, gifts and skills. Look for ways for your spouse to shine, and always be the biggest cheerleader for each other.

Scripture

Now the Lord God said, It is not good (sufficient, satisfactory) that the man should be alone; I will make him a helper meet (suitable, adapted, complementary) for him. (Genesis 2:18 AMPC)

Exercise

Take a moment this week and write five strengths, skills or talents your spouse has. Encourage them to find ways to use these God-given abilities.

Affirmation

My spouse is the best gift that God has given me. I treasure my spouse and love her/him with unconditional love. Together we are a powerful team. We appreciate each other's strengths, abilities and expertise. We celebrate each other's talents, gifts and skills. We are not threatened by each other's strength, but we learn to depend on each other's expertise. We rejoice with each other's abilities and together look for ways make each other shine. We will always be the biggest cheerleader for each other.

Prayer

Lord, we exalt and magnify your name today. Thank you for the gift of my amazing spouse. In Genesis 2:18 you said, *"It is not good (sufficient, satisfactory) that the man should be alone; I will make him a helper meet (suitable, adapted, complementary) for him." (AMPC)* We ask that you will fortify and strengthen us as a mature couple whose focus is on completing and not competing. We ask that you will give us the wisdom and grace to fulfill the things that our spouse says is important to them. Father, release your grace and favor over us as a couple and cause us to grow by the power of the Holy Spirit.

Week 20

Don't be a taker

If you are not bringing value to your spouse, if your presence in their life is not making them better and feel special, your spouse will find ways to spend as little time with you as possible. No one likes to be used.

Tip

Many people enter into a relationship with an expectation to be served happiness. First of all, the primary call of a husband or wife is to serve their spouse. Secondly, no one can make you happy. Happiness is a feeling about the current circumstances. Things change in people and in life. (One man was unhappy in his marriage because his wife no longer had the sexy shape she had when she was younger and before she had *his* children. "I am just not attracted to her anymore.") Your marriage will go through different seasons, but the love of God is consistent through every season. Much of what people are expecting from each other can only be provided by God. God has to fill your heart before you can bring value to your spouse.

Scripture

It is not conceited (arrogant and inflated with pride); it is not rude (unmannerly) and does not act unbecomingly. ***Love (God's love in us) does not insist on its own rights or its own way, for it is not self-seeking;*** *it is not touchy or fretful or resentful; it takes no account of the evil done to it [it pays no attention to a suffered wrong]. (1 Corinthians 13:5 AMPC, emphasis added)*

Exercise

Ask your spouse this question: What are two things that are important to you in a relationship? Write them down and make it your aim to provide those top two priorities. Also purchase the book, *His Needs, Her Needs*, and make this a book-reading project. Make it your aim to meet the top two needs in your spouse's life.

Affirmation

We are not takers but big givers. We bring value to each other in many ways, such as acts of service, preferring one another, and giving gifts and quality time. We spend as much time as possible with each other just because we like each other. We never treat our spouse in a demeaning manner or make them feel unimportant. Much of what people are expecting from each other can only be provided by God. Our marriage will go through different seasons, but the love of God is consistent through every season. Father God, we release your love in our hearts and will choose to bring value to each other.

Prayer

Father, all blessings and honor and glory belong to you. Craft in us an enormous desire to bring value to our marriage. When we are together, my spouse becomes a better person. Father, we ask that you will continue to touch our lives with your good hand of blessing so we can experience the God kind of joy for one another. We humble ourselves before you and take authority over selfishness and self-seeking. We take authority over conceited, arrogant and prideful attitudes that may be lurking inside of us. We choose not to be rude, unmannerly and unbecoming. Father, sharpen us and soften our hearts to become spouses that keep on giving.

Week 21

In-laws or outlaws?

When you married your spouse, you also married into their family. If they have a healthy family, then you married into a healthy family; if they have a dysfunctional family, then you married into that dysfunction. You will have to navigate through whatever you married into.

Tip

First and foremost, you have to *leave* your family and *cleave* to your spouse. This is an issue of priority. You cannot build a unified marriage if you don't let go of family relationships to form a new union. Yes, you love your family, and you still relate to your family, but not at the same level. Your first circle of intimacy is your spouse and your children, then your mom, dad, and siblings. If you get this out of order, you set yourself up for failure.

Many families *impose* their will on your new union. Just think of a typical marriage event and how drama generally arises when you are trying your best to have a wonderful and peaceful marriage ceremony. Many families are so selfish; they don't consider this is the most important event of your life, other than accepting Jesus. So often the family is so focused on what they want, that they are completely oblivious to your needs and how their behavior is making you feel.

Put your spouse first, and your family second, or you can just marry your family!

Scripture

Therefore a man shall leave his father and his mother and shall become united and cleave to his wife, and they shall become one flesh. (Genesis 2:24 AMPC)

Exercise

Have a conversation about in-laws. What do you each expect of each other in this area? Write down a set of values in this area. **Example 1:** I will not talk to my mom about things going on in my marriage and belittle my spouse. (This, of course, does not include forms of abuse.) **Example 2:** I will not decide on my family's request without talking to my spouse about it. These are just two of many examples. Set expectations in this area and agree on them.

Affirmation

First and foremost, we *leave* our family and *cleave* to our spouse. This is our priority. We will not keep family and in-laws in the midst of our marriage. We understand what it means to leave our family and cleave to each other.

We keep the first circle of intimacy with each other and never allow our parents or siblings to enter into our personal space. We examine our relationships with our family to correct any unhealthy relationships that interfere with our intimacy with each other. In the name of Jesus, we rebuke and drive out of our marriage family displacement and dysfunction that will hinder our marriage unity. We cleave with a passion for each other, and we leave family so that we truly become *one flesh*.

Prayer

Father, thank you for leading our marriage into the pathway of peace. We stand on Genesis 2:24, *"Therefore a man shall leave his father and his mother and shall become united and cleave to his wife, and they shall become one flesh." (AMPC)* Lord, give us wisdom when talking with family (moms), so we will not communicate issues in our marriage and belittle our spouse. Give us the courage to seek a professional person if we are struggling with abuse in any area. We will rely on your help, Lord, not to decide on a family request without talking to our spouse about it first. We choose to submit to your Word. Bless us and empower us to succeed.

Week 22

Who's first?

Who is going to be first to love, first to serve, first to forgive? It is a necessary attitude in a healthy marriage. Usually, it is who is going to hold out the longest, be angry first, won't speak, etc. That leads to a lot of sleeping on the couch at night. This makes no sense when you married the person of your dreams, does it?

Tip

Instead of who's going to be angry the longest, sit down and talk about *why* you chose to spend your life together in the first place. Your "why" should be big enough to resolve your issues once you know you why it should be big enough to resolve issues quickly!

Scripture

And let us consider how to stir up one another to love and good works. (Hebrews 10:24 ESV)

And let us consider one another to provoke unto love and to good works. (Hebrews 10:24 KJV)

However, let each man of you [without exception] love his wife as [being in a sense] his very own self; and let the wife see that she respects and reverences her husband [that she notices him, regards him, honors him, prefers him, venerates, and esteems him; and that she defers to him, praises him, and loves and admires him exceedingly]. (Ephesians 5:33 AMPC)

Exercise

Review the fruit of the Spirit found in Galatians 5:22-23 – *"But the fruit of the Spirit is love, joy, peace, patience, kindness, goodness, faithfulness, gentleness, self-control; against such things there is no law." (ESV)* As you review these verses together, compliment each other on how you have walked in the Spirit over a recent issue. Talk about the impact that is having on your relationship and how this is also empowering your children to have successful relationships in the future.

Affirmation

We are going to be first to love, first to serve and the first to forgive. This is the only attitude we will have in our marriage. We will never be stubborn, hard-headed, unwilling to change or be the last to apologize. There will be zero nights sleeping on the couch for us, because we act on the Word of God to love and do something good for each other. We are fulfilling our greatest dreams together because we stir each other up to love. We challenge ourselves every day to love bigger, harder, longer and with more excitement for each other.

Prayer

Father God, we will give praise and honor to your name, O Lord Most High. *"My mouth is filled with your praise, declaring your splendor all day long." (Psalm 71:8 NIV)* Shower upon us your unwavering love and compassion, equipping us to love and good works all day long. It is in your presence that your anointing will come upon our lives and break every chain and yoke of bondage. We both operate in the first to love, first to serve and the first to forgive principles of God. We practice your Word which says, *"However, let each man of you [without exception] love his wife as [being in a sense] his very own self; and let the wife see that she respects and reverences her husband [that she notices him, regards him, honors him, prefers him, venerates, and esteems him; and that she defers to him, praises him, and loves and admires him exceedingly]." (Ephesians 5:33 AMPC)*

Week 23

Grow together

If you don't grow together, you grow apart.

Tip

Growth is not automatic—it's systematic. The only way to overcome issues in your marriage is to grow out of them. Growth must be stimulated through a series of purposeful and intentional activities. In other words, there must be a *plan* to grow.

Scripture

Like newborn babies you should crave (thirst for, earnestly desire) the pure (unadulterated) spiritual milk, that by it you may be nurtured and grow unto [completed] salvation. (1 Peter 2:2 AMPC)

Exercise

Starting with your spiritual life, think about how can you improve *together* through Bible reading, study, memorization, meditation, affirmation. You can hold each other accountable here. What about your prayer life? Pray together about important issues in your lives once per week. (Start with five minutes and grow from there.) Look at a few other areas that are important to your marriage health: finances, communication, health, children, etc.

Develop a plan to grow. Don't do too much and too many at a time. Pace yourself and be consistent.

Affirmation

Because growth is not automatic, we challenge ourselves to grow through applying effective principles of growth in our lives. We declare that we are growing so big that our issues disappear completely. We are not arrogant, stubborn and "stuck on stupid" to where we will not even ask for help or agree to use any help outside of ourselves. We eagerly commit quality time together to grow bigger than our issues. We declare the Word of God is the final authority. We align ourselves to various resources, Bible reading, affirmation, meditating on scriptures, reading books, etc. We systematically grow bigger with God.

Prayer

Oh, magnify the Lord, for he is worthy to be praised. Father, our prayer today is that we would grow more and more into the image of Jesus, your Son. The purpose Jesus came down to the earth was to destroy the works of the devil in our lives. Through the power of your blood, Jesus, cleanse us from negative thinking and deadly words we have spoken in the past. In the mighty name of Jesus negative and painful words of destruction, leave us now. Father, give us a fresh start as we walk in humility towards one another, committing to the progress of growing until it changes us for good. Father, growth is painful, but we say, "Bring on the pain."

Week 24

No single friends

Being married requires a new set of friends. The people closest to you determine your success. If you want to have a successful marriage, build a relationship with successful couples or others like yourself who want what you want.

Tip

Some couples try to maintain relationships with single people, and even some will try to maintain a relationship with a single of the opposite sex. *Hello!* I don't think so! Or even worse, hanging out with divorcees? Now, you need to be kind and loving to everybody, but your inner circle *must* be comprised of the people that can help you get to your destination. Tough choices to make, but if you want a thriving marriage, you must *upgrade* your friends.

Scripture

Where there is no guidance, a people fall, but in an abundance of counselors there is safety. (Proverbs 11:14 ESV)

Where there is no counsel, purposes are frustrated, but with many counselors they are accomplished. (Proverbs15:22 AMPC)

Exercise

Take an inventory of the closest friends in your life. How many of them are in successful marriages? Identify new relationships you can form this year. Look for three types of marriages. Up—Look for marriages that are more successful than yours. Across—Look for marriages that are experiencing similar challenges, but actively working on improving their relationship. Down—Look for marriages of less than a year with younger couples you can mentor. Now, you don't have to do this all at the same time, but this is the goal. Take small steps.

Affirmation

We look "Across" for couples whose marriages are experiencing similar challenges. And "Down" for marriages of less than a year with younger couples we can mentor. We don't hang out with divorcees, because we are looking for couples who can lift our marriage to the next level. Our inner circle is comprised of couples who can help us get to our destination, which is a happy, successful, long-lasting marriage. We are not complacent and mediocre in our pursuit of a successful marriage, so we are constantly upgrading our friends when necessary.

Prayer

Father, we seek first the your kingdom and your righteousness, and all things will be added to us. We believe your Word that says, *"Where there is no counsel, purposes are frustrated, but with many counselors, they are accomplished." (Proverbs15:22 AMPC)* We ask that you open our eyes of understanding so we are willing to move forward with embracing friends who will enhance us. Guide us to add other couples in our life who are more established in their marriage, couples who are experiencing the same issues and couples whom we can mentor. We ask that you lead us by your Spirit to develop these meaningful relationships that will help us grow and sharpen our marriage union.

Week 25

Substance abuse

Here are a couple of statements from a 2016 substance abuse and marriage statistics publication: "Couples Who Abuse Substances More Likely to Get Divorced" and "Increased Alcohol Consumption Increases Divorce Rates."

If your spouse is dealing with substance abuse in your marriage, you must empower your spouse rather than enable them.

Tip

The first step to address this issue is to pray for your spouse. That's a great start, but this will require some additional action. "Action" is the key word—don't bury your head in the sand and hope it will just go away. However, all you can do is provide the opportunity for your spouse to address their addiction. You can't *make* them do something about it. But, you can certainly apply loving pressure by not enabling them to continue without consequences—even as far as a legal separation, if necessary. If they want to destroy themselves, you can't go down with them, especially if you have children. Some spouses may even get into illegal and criminal behavior that could endanger you and your family, so this is something that must be addressed. The next step would be to seek marriage counseling that specializes in substance abuse issues. Lastly, having a small circle of friends you can confide in and can support you through this process would be ideal.

Scripture

Little children, you are from God and have overcome them, for he who is in you is greater than he who is in the world. (1 John 4:4 ESV)

Exercise

Using the prayer section of this topic, take this matter before the Lord. Identify two to three potential substance abuse and marriage counselors. Interview them to determine the right fit for you. It is always good to talk with marriage counselors who are actually married—and have good marriages. Don't feel like you're being intrusive by asking specific questions: How long have you been married? Why did you choose to be a counselor in this area? Do you have clients who are willing to share their success stories as a result of working with you? This is a great start in addressing this issue in your marriage.

Affirmation

We are open and honest with each other concerning strongholds in our life. If my spouse is dealing with substance abuse in our marriage, we decide to empower each other rather than enable one another. We are under the shadow of the Almighty, and we do not allow ourselves to be controlled by a substance like alcohol or drugs. Substance abuse will not dominate and control our lives. Jesus is Lord of Lords and King of Kings. We surrender every part of our lives to him. Satan comes to kill steal and destroy, but Jesus has come to give us life more abundantly. We decree the verse that says, *"Little children, you are from God and have overcome them, for he who is in you is greater than he who is in the world." (1 John 4:4 ESV)*

Prayer

Jesus, we will trust in you with all our heart and lean not on our own understanding; in all our ways we will acknowledge you, and you will make our paths straight. We will not be wise in our own eyes, but we will fear the LORD and eschew evil. This will bring health to our body and nourishment to our bones. Father, we will not sin against you or each other by allowing ourselves to become victims of substance abuse. We know that the thief comes to bring destruction in our life and marriage, but greater is he that is in us than he that is in the world. Father God, move in our marriage so that if my spouse is dealing with substance abuse, set them free now. Put in my spouse a desire to deal with all issues. Give me wisdom and strength not to bury my head and become an enabler but to address the issues, pray and seek professional help.

A Marriage Investment Story . . .

Teamwork

I received the Lord at age 15 and accepted the call to preach the Gospel of Jesus at 16. It was Jesus and me every day. I learn to follow him and stay true to his Word. Now I was newly married, after two years (I was 22) we were really beginning to grow together. Sandra was no longer a baby Christian. Plus, she had experience in life as a 33-year-old woman.

During a time of fellowship, the Spirit said, "You are used to hearing from me and moving forward with your life. But you are married now, and you have to learn how to be a team. If you continue to work alone, you will do well, but if you will bring your wife along with you and work as a team, you will accomplish ten times more. From this point on, do not do anything without your wife's full agreement. Make sure she knows everything you know, reads everything you read—work together, and you will excel!"

That was a powerful word from the Lord. I call it God's supernatural math, one plus one equals ten! Sandra and I do everything together; I would not have it any other way. She is smart, and she knows how to hear from God. She also helps cover my blind spots. We all have them. We have to learn to complement each other.

Week 26

Marriage checkup

Don't assume your spouse is happy, don't assume your marriage is in great shape, *ask*!

Tip

Everyone understands the importance of a health checkup. Shouldn't a marriage checkup be just as important? A marriage checkup is a great way to course correct any issues you may be dealing with and keep your one flesh process on track. The key, though, is to speak the truth in love without your spouse reacting with judgment toward you and justification for his/her actions. *Just listen please!*

Scripture

*Rather, **speaking the truth in love**, we are to grow up in every way into him who is the head, into Christ. (Ephesians 4:15 ESV, emphasis added)*

Exercise

Use our marriage threat assessment survey (www.MarriageEquitySystems.com) and follow the recommended steps to improve in the areas that threaten the health and peace of your marriage.

Affirmation

My spouse and I make sure we have marriage check-ups on a regular basis. We do not take each other for granted and assume our spouse is happy. We use our marriage checkup to guarantee we are securing a life of happiness and peace. We are growing, maturing and learning how to not let the "issues with each other become the mission." We evaluate areas in our marriage that cause contention and use scriptures to overcome these areas that can potentially bring total destruction in our pursuit of a lasting marriage. We don't just grin and bear through the pain, but we are proactive and fully engaged to drive negativity out of our marriage.

Prayer

Father, pour out the power of your love on us today. Empower us through the help of the Holy Spirit to love each other more and better than ever before. Cultivate and develop us into the loving couple whose desire is to please and serve each other better than the days, weeks and years before. We desire that through your leading we are living the God kind of marriage—a marriage filled with love, understanding and peace. For in your presence, Lord, there is the fullness of joy. Let your grace and wisdom come upon us each day as we surrender to your will. Teach us how to address the difficult issues in love and not display anger, bitterness and malice. We will follow your plan into developing the greatest love for each other. Show us how to fully walk in your perfect way. We are committed to activating this verse – *"Rather, speaking the truth in love, we are to grow up in every way into him who is the head, into Christ." (Ephesians 4:15 ESV)*

Week 27

Mama's boy

Nobody wants a man who is still nursing! Mama needs to "get a life" and baby boy needs to "get a wife"!

Tip

Mama said, "Boy, when I gave birth to you, I almost died! You owe me!" No, you owe your mama love and respect, but she cannot be first in your life. This spot is *only* for your wife. Don't think you can go around talking about "my mama this" and "my mama that," and "Mama's food is better," and "Mama does it like this." First, no woman wants to be compared to your mama! Dude, chill out! Mama can also treat your wife like she is *never* good enough for her baby. This can cause serious issues in your marriage. Remember, the key here is you must *leave* your mama and *cleave* to your wife. Otherwise, you will never be one flesh. Your mama can't make you the man she needs in her life—that time is past. You must live in a way that you honor your mom for the life she provided for you and at the same time grow in intimacy with your wife and assure her that she is always first.

Scripture

"…Therefore a man shall leave his father and his mother and hold fast to his wife, and the two shall become one flesh…" (Matthew 19:4-5 ESV)

Exercise

Have a conversation with your wife about how she feels about you and your mama. Listen closely without a verbal smackdown. Ask her what you can do to improve things in this area. If things are great, then ask what can you do better.

Affirmation

I am not a mama's boy, and my wife didn't marry a mama's boy! Regardless, my mama needs to get a life because I have a wonderful wife. When my mom says, "You owe me," I let her know I only owe her love and respect, but she cannot be first in my life. My wife is first in my life, and she always will be. I decree from this day forward I will not use words to exalt my mama over my wife. I am not a mama's boy. If I have been a mama's boy, today marks the last day for being a mama's boy. My wife is first from now on. My spouse and I have an open conversation about my mom to make sure I am never putting my mom first.

Prayer

Father God, help me to walk in wisdom concerning putting my wife first before my mama and all family. I love my mama and always will, but now I have a wife. Teach me to honor my mom and not operate as a mama's boy. I despise every attribute of a mama's boy behavior, so I will not allow mama's whining to pull me into putting her first. Thank you for blessing me with an amazing wife who can never be compared to my mother. As a man, I will honor your Word and cleave passionately to my wife. I realize my mama's assignment was to prepare me for my wife, "*... Therefore a man shall leave his father and his mother and hold fast to his wife, and the two shall become one flesh...*" *(Matthew19:4-5 ESV)* I am cleaving to my Boo! Father heal painful hurts that have created a breach in our marriage. Show me how to put my wife first.

Week 28

Daddy's girl

Definition of a daddy's girl: A girl (adult or child) who has a strong bond with her father, typically the bond to her father is stronger than the bond to her mother and her husband. A daddy's girl compares her husband to her dad in a way that he is intimidated by her dad.

Tip

Don't compare your husband to your dad. I know your dad is awesome, but your man needs admiration from you to breathe. Talking up your dad tends to belittle your man. Also, your dad is not the head of your home, your husband is. Remember the Word teaches to *leave* your mother and *father* and *cleave* to your husband. God's goal is always *one flesh*.

Scripture

"...Therefore a man shall leave his father and his mother and hold fast to his wife, and the two shall become one flesh..." (Matthew 19:4-5 ESV)

Exercise

Have a conversation with your husband about your dad. How does he feel about your relationship with your dad? Does he feel threatened, or embraced?

Affirmation

I am not a daddy's girl. We observe the Word of God that says, *"...Therefore a man shall leave his father and his mother and hold fast to his wife, and the two shall become one flesh..." (Matthew 19:4-5 ESV)* I respect my husband, who is head of our home, and I never do anything to make him feel less than my super-hero. Regardless of how my dad wants to still see me as his little girl, I will not yield to this childish behavior. My husband and I agree that there is no daddy's girl living in this house. I will always love and respect my daddy; however, the days of daddy's little girl have come and gone. Bye, daddy's little girl!

Prayer

We give all the glory to the Lord of Lords, the great I AM, the way, the truth and the life. Thank you, Father, that I can come boldly before your throne of grace and receive help in time of need. I am moving and celebrating my marriage with the man of my dreams, and being a daddy's girl is not part of the dream you have for us. I will honor respect and always put my husband before my daddy. Thank you, Father, for giving me the courage to be a wife and not embrace being a daddy's girl. As for me and my man, we will cleave to each other and leave mom and dad's house. Bye, daddy's girl; hello, wonderful wife.

Week 29

Unity in spiritual growth

Spiritual growth is paramount in your life. However, nothing is more powerful than a husband and wife growing together.

Tip

Spiritual growth is the root system of everything God desires to do in your life. However, growth is not automatic but systematic. By growing together, you establish a pattern of success for your marriage union. As we abide in Christ, fruitfulness in your spiritual journey is the result. When you make spiritual growth as a couple a priority, this ensures your growth in all areas. You will, therefore, grow closer together instead of growing apart.

Scripture

Blessed is the man that walketh not in the counsel of
the wicked,
Nor standeth in the way of sinners,
Nor sitteth in the seat of the scornful.
But his delight is in the law of the Lord;
And in his law doth he meditates day and night.
And he shall be like a tree planted by the
streams of water,
That bringeth forth its fruit in its season,

Whose leaf also doth not wither;

And whatsoever he doeth shall prosper. (Psalm 1:1-4 KJV)

Exercise

Here are the key areas where you need to grow spiritually as a couple:

- **Prayer**—determine a regular time to meet the daily and once per week as a couple.
- **The Word**—use a Bible reading program.
- **Key areas of development**—discuss an area in which you would like to grow together, such as fruit of the Spirit, forgiveness, hearing God's voice, etc.

Write the plan down and share this with another couple for accountability.

Affirmation

My spouse and I are growing more and more in unity every day. Unity and spiritual growth is our passion. We spend quality time going through resources, praying and reading the Word, which will catapult us into a deeper unity with one another. Spiritual growth is paramount in our desire to reach a level of unity that cannot be fragmented. Our unity and spiritual growth make us one dynamic power couple. We recognize that growth is not automatic but systematic, so we endeavor to systematically grow regularly. Spiritual growth determines the root system of the success of our marriage. Therefore, our focus is on growing together. Spending time in the Word will make us like a tree planted by the rivers of water whose leaves (our marriage) will not wither. We will prosper in everything we do and find other couples we can share our success with.

Prayer

We will give thanks to the Lord, for he is good, for his love endures forever. Thank you, Father God, that your good hand of blessing is watching over our marriage. We are blessed because we choose not to walk in the counsel of the ungodly, we do not stand in the way of sinners, and we do not sit in the seat of the scornful, but our delight is in the law of the Lord and in your law we meditate day and night. We shall be like a tree planted by the rivers of water. Father God, surround us with your lovingkindness, and tender mercies so that we will be strengthened. With your help, Lord Jesus, we are growing and establishing a pattern of success for our marriage.

Week 30

See no good

It is so easy to focus on the negative traits of your spouse. If you look for the negative, you will find it.

Tip

A critical fault-finding attitude is like bug repellent. Nobody wants to be around a person that makes them feel bad about themselves. So, if you want to drive your spouse away from you, this is the way to do it. Instead of finding fault and magnifying the bad, look for the good and celebrate the beautiful! Encouragement lifts a person's belief in themselves, and consistent encouragement will impact behavior.

Scripture

Let no foul or polluting language, nor evil word nor unwholesome or worthless talk [ever] come out of your mouth, but only such [speech] as is good and beneficial to the spiritual progress of others, as is fitting to the need and the occasion, that it may be a blessing and give grace (God's favor) to those who hear it. (Ephesians 4:29 AMPC)

Exercise

Get a sheet of paper and list ten *positive* traits about your spouse. Share your results. Make it your aim to celebrate what is good about your spouse.

Affirmation

My spouse and I focus on seeing the good in each other. We never focus on the imperfections, idiosyncrasies, irritating quirks and anything that can be an irritation to each other. Focusing on negativity is not going to build a healthy marriage. We desire to strengthen and build each other up as we grow together. We meditate on scriptures that will build our spirit, mind and emotions. We confess Ephesians 4:29 daily – *"Let no foul or polluting language, nor evil word nor unwholesome or worthless talk [ever] come out of our mouths, but only such [speech] as is good and beneficial to the spiritual progress of others, as is fitting to the need and the occasion, that it may be a blessing and give grace (God's favor) to those who hear it." (AMPC)* The Word of God is changing us from strength to strength. Instead of finding fault and magnifying the bad, we look for the good and celebrate the beautiful! We encourage and liven each other up to keep our atmosphere full of love and good feelings for one another.

Prayer

Father, we worship you, for your Word says, *"Yours, Lord, is the greatness and the power and the glory and the majesty and the splendor, for everything in heaven and earth is yours." (1 Chronicles 29:11a NIV)* We offer sacrifices and praise to your name as we surrender to your plan for our marriage. Anoint our eyes, ears and mouth so we will see and say only good things. We repent to one another, for being critical and having a fault-finding, abusive, destructive, attitude that eats away and undermines the foundation of our unity. We commit ourselves to practice your Word in our speech, actions and attitudes. We will walk in love, forgiveness, and kindness every day of our life together. We will not allow foul polluting language or evil words or unwholesome talk to come out of our mouth. Lord Jesus, equip us to do your Word with all of our heart.

A Marriage Investment Story . . .

You are a wonderful wife

Sandra was going through a season of depression. She laid on the couch most of the day. She was there on the couch when I left, and she was there when I got home from work. Two of my children were still at home. My children were in pajamas when I left and when I came back. Meals were late and no sex at night! I was frustrated. So I would exercise to relieve my frustration. Of course, the enemy is right there whispering in my ear to be harsh with Sandra. I sought the Lord about it, and he told me to tell Sandra every day, "Sandra you are a wonderful wife, and you are a wonderful mother." I was to do this daily before I went to work.

He said, "Don't say anything about what she is not doing. Just tell her what I told you to say."

"But Lord, that is not true! Look at the house, look at the kids, look at how she is neglecting me!"

The Spirit said, "Tell her these words every day!" So I did. Later, Sandra recalled she would think about what I told her all day long. Why would he say this?

I followed the Lord until it healed my wife. Words are so powerful and love never fails. She has always been a wonderful wife and a wonderful mother, but she needed God to heal her from depression through my words.

Week 31

Encouragement

You cannot encourage your spouse too much. The more you give it, the better it feels and the more it is needed.

Tip

Create an environment and culture of encouragement in your marriage. We live in a world of negativity. People lust to hear the dirt, the failures, the scandals of others. It is like in the time of the gladiators. People love carnage. They love to see the mutilation of others. So to live in an environment of encouragement is so rare, but it is an amazing place to be! Your relationship with each other can be that of encouragement. Agree to build each other up and never tear each other down. It's great to practice this publicly, but it's even greater to practice it privately. Everybody wants to *feel* good about themselves. So make it your aim for your spouse to *feel* good about themselves when they are with you. Encouragement from your very thoughts about each other is the direct line to this outcome!

Scripture

Therefore encourage (admonish, exhort) one another and edify (strengthen and build up) one another, just as you are doing. (1 Thessalonians 5:11 AMPC)

Exercise

Think of ways you can encourage each other. What skills and talents does your spouse have? What goals and dreams does your spouse desire to fulfill? What difficult challenges does your spouse face? What failures did your spouse experience in the past? What fears does your spouse have about future dreams? Discuss these and write this in a journal or log. First, pray over them. Ask God how you can help your sweetheart. Follow the Holy Spirit in inspiring and encouraging them in each area for a season. Build them up and strengthen their faith. They will love you the more for it. Be your spouse's CEO—Chief Encouragement Officer!

Affirmation

We are a growing couple. Regardless whether we've been married five years or 40, we spend time encouraging each other. We can never encourage each other enough, so we use every opportunity we get to encourage each other. The more we do it, the better it feels and the more it is needed. We create an environment and culture of encouragement in our marriage. We do not allow ourselves to be negative and critical of each other. We live in a world of negativity where people lust to hear the dirt, the failures, the scandals of others. Therefore we refuse to follow after this negative mindset. We keep this scripture before us – *"Therefore encourage (admonish, exhort) one another and edify (strengthen and build up) one another, just as you are doing." (1 Thessalonians 5:11 AMPC)* We agree to build each other up and never tear each other down. We practice this whenever we are together, especially in private where it matters most.

Prayer

Praise be to the God and Father of our Lord Jesus Christ, the Father of compassion and the God of all comfort, who comforts us in all our troubles so that we can comfort those in any trouble with the comfort we receive from God. Father God, you are the God of compassion and comfort, and you can help us to create an environment and culture of encouragement in our marriage. Strengthen us to overcome immaturity, rudeness, selfishness and self-seeking behavior. We cry out to you and ask that you guide us as a couple into loving one another unconditionally. Open our eyes and let us see the power of positive words, for life and death are in the power of the tongue. We choose to use our tongues as vessels of honor and not dishonor towards each other. You said therefore encourage, exhort and strengthen one another. Let my spouse never become overwhelmed with difficult challenges. Through teamwork, support and encouragement we can overcome every obstacle.

Week 32

Fighting together

Who wants to be alone when you are in the fight of your life? Everybody wants a "foxhole partner." So fighting together is a fight that is impossible to lose! Even if you lose a battle, you will win the war!

Tip

Rather than fighting each other, *fight together* against a mutual enemy or obstacle. Now that's a fight worth fighting for! When you fight each other, everyone loses. When you fight together, everyone wins, even if you lose the fight. You are better because you came together over an issue or obstacle. Fighting together strengthens the character of your marriage, the love you have for each other and the hope you have for your future together. Fighting each other is *self-mutilation* or *cutting*. We are admonished to love each other and warned against fighting in the body of Christ. How much more is this true in a marriage union. *"For the whole law is fulfilled in one word: 'You shall love your neighbor as yourself.' But if you bite and devour one another, watch out that you are not consumed by one another." (Galatians 5:14-15 ESV)* It sounds like cannibalism to me.

Scripture

You shall chase your enemies, and they shall fall before you by the sword. Five of you shall chase a hundred, and a hundred of you shall chase ten thousand, and your enemies shall fall before you by the sword. (Leviticus 26:7-8 ESV)

Again I say to you, if two of you agree on earth about anything they ask, it will be done for them by my Father in heaven. (Matthew 18:19 ESV)

Exercise

Think about some of the greatest challenges you have in your marriage. Is it health, finances, business, children, etc.? We are talking about something affecting the peace of your marriage. First, identify one giant at a time. Then find scripture that promises your victory in that area. Build your faith through the Word and write out a prayer using the scripture you have selected. (Note: Personalize the scripture by placing we, us, etc. in the place of the words referring to the subject.) You can even insert your name. "John and Sandra are more than conquerors…" If necessary seek coaching or talk to a couple that are experiencing victory in the area you are fighting for victory.

Affirmation

My spouse and I agree to walk in unity. We would rather fight together than fight each other when we meet our enemy. Fighting each other is self-mutilation or cutting. We will not allow the enemy to turn us against each other, because we love each other and our union. To allow division just separates us. No one wants to be alone when you are in a fight for your life. So we join our faith together and fight together to win the battle. We thank God that we are in the foxhole together and not alone. My spouse and I are committed, faithful and strategic partners for one another—when one is down the other one will pick them up. We stand on Matthew 18:19 – *"Again I say to you, if two of you agree on earth about anything they ask, it will be done for them by my Father in heaven." (ESV)* God, it says whatever we ask in agreement together in prayer. Therefore we make sure we are walking in unity, love and forgiveness. We are better because we came together over issues or obstacles. We will fight together, strengthening the character of our marriage. We submit ourselves to God and resist the devil, knowing he will flee from us.

Prayer

"The LORD is the everlasting God, the Creator of the ends of the earth. He does not faint or grow weary; his understanding is unsearchable. He gives power to the faint, and to him who has no might he increases strength." (Isaiah 40:28-29 ESV) Father, we stand and fight against the enemy. The weapons of our warfare are not carnal, but they're mighty through God to the pulling down strongholds in our marriage. We believe and receive answers to prayers. We choose not to fight each other, but we choose to fight together against issues that affect our health, finances,

business, children, etc. We stand on your Word in Leviticus 26:7-8 and say we shall chase our enemies, and they shall fall before us by the sword. Five of us shall chase a hundred, and a hundred of us shall chase ten thousand, and our enemies shall fall before us by the sword. Because two are better than one, even if we lose the battle we will always win the war. Father, strengthen us so we will stand and become more united and stronger in every way.

Week 33

Expectation

Expectation is a strong belief that something will happen or be the case in the future. What do you expect in a relationship? What expectation, if not met, is a "deal breaker"?

Tip

Many issues arise in a marriage because of unstated expectations. You expected something of your spouse, and they did not deliver. So, disappointment sets in. Now, it is possible that your spouse did not know what you were expecting or did not realize how important this was to you. Therefore, it is vital that you communicate what you expect in your marriage. Share what level of priority this is to you, so there is a clear understanding of its importance. Some unmet expectations are "deal breakers," and some are not. Your spouse needs to know the difference. Whatever you expect of your spouse, be sure you are willing to do the same. And are doing first. Otherwise, your relationship is headed for a win/lose scenario.

Scripture

*Rather, **speaking the truth in love**, we are to grow up in every way into him who is the head, into Christ. (Ephesians 4:15 ESV, emphasis added)*

Exercise

Sit down as a couple and allow each of you to communicate what a happy and fulfilling marriage looks like to you. Please allow your spouse to share *without* interruption and weird body language (breathing, facial expression, folding arms, etc.). Some people will not share what they really feel if they are punished for being honest. Without honesty and openness, you have no relationship. It's *fake*, and it won't last.

Determine the priority level of your spouse's expectation and discuss if you can meet that or not. There are times in a relationship that *compromise* is necessary. You can't always get everything you want. So talk it over and come to a consensus. Take turns until the core expectations are settled. Pray together about your plan, and ask the Holy Spirit to help you execute your plan.

Affirmation

We choose to communicate reasonable expectations. We do not have issues in our marriage because of unstated expectations. We are open and honest with each other as we communicate our expectations in a manner that can be received. We do not use abrasive, rude, inconsiderate language when communicating with each other. We will pray over our expectations. We realize without God it is impossible to have a harmonious, happy relationship, so we keep God in the center of our marriage and allow him to teach us how to meet each other's needs.

Prayer

"The LORD reigns, let the nations tremble; he sits enthroned between the cherubim, let the earth shake. Great is the LORD in Zion; he is exalted over all the nations. Let them praise your great and awesome name—he is holy." (Psalm 99:1-3 NIV) Father, we ask that you will mature us and strengthen us as we share our expectations. Give us grace and understanding as we share. Father, search our hearts and remove any hindrances and erroneous beliefs concerning each other. We will not use this time to belittle and criticize each other. We will not allow the enemy to get a foothold in our marriage because of fear of how it will be received. Father, help us to not explode in anger, frustration or become demanding when we don't see our expectations being met. We understand that it takes time to develop in our marriage, so we will allow time for the expectations to grow and develop.

Week 34

Foundational Core Values™

Foundational Core Values™ is a concrete, values-based decision-making process; it helps people unplug from emotionalism and plug into their values-based system as they engage the world around them.

Tip

"Values are the rules by which you live, and become the basis for how you judge yourself and the world around you." This is especially critical as it relates to a life-long marriage union. I think we can all agree that emotionally based relationships have taken their toll on our lives. Though it is important that you have "feelings" for your spouse, feelings *cannot* be the foundation of your life together. Because feelings are so "wishy-washy," you cannot build a solid life on feelings alone. You need something much deeper. You need foundational core values to drive your relationship. Values-based decision making is a secure, safe way to build a life that is consistent with Biblical principles and allows you to connect with your spouse on multiple levels. Through these "connections" you can create a clear, direct path to the one-flesh idea found in scripture.

Scripture

I can do all things through him who strengthens me. (Philippians 4:13 ESV)

Exercise

Each of you should take the Foundational Core Values™ free assessment:

https://FoundationalCoreValues.com/free-assessment/

Be sure to watch the video first and follow instructions *exactly*. From this exercise, you will discover your foundational core values. It will take a few weeks to complete the process, so be patient. Hold each other accountable as you follow through with this discovery process. After you complete this assessment and determine your five foundational core values, write a short sentence about what each value means to you. Share this with each other and find where you can connect with each other. This is a good start to building a life based upon values-based decision making instead of emotionally based decision making.

Affirmation

We can do all things through Jesus Christ who gives us strength. We establish concrete values in that are not based upon emotions and feelings. Our core values become the basis for how we judge ourselves and the world around us. We will have a long successful marriage implementing our core values and enjoying each other.

We do not allow our feelings and emotions, which are wishy-washy, to dominate and control the outcome of our marriage equity. We will take the time to go over the Foundational Core Values™ assessment test, follow the instructions and watch the video to start connecting from our foundational core values providers. After we complete this assessment and determine our five foundation core values, we will write a short sentence of what each value means to us. We will share this with each other and find where we can connect with each other. We are building a life based upon values-based decision making instead of emotions-based decision making.

Prayer

Father God, we praise you with our whole heart. *"Let all that I am praise the Lord; with my whole heart, I will praise His holy name. Let all that I am praise the Lord; may I never forget the good things He does for me. He forgives all my sins and heals all my diseases. He redeems me from death and crowns me with love and tender mercies." (Psalm 103:1-4 NLT)* Father God, thank you for helping us to walk in our foundational core values. We will establish concrete values based upon decision making in our marriage. Yes, we will make decisions concerning foundational core values. Lead us beside the still waters and the quiet resting places. Restore our soul, mind, will and any emotions so that we can make values-based decisions in our marriage. Give us wisdom and insight as we discover values and rules by which we live our lives every day. Father, show us the importance of how core values are critical in our marriage union. Living our lives with these Foundational Core Values™ will strengthen our marriage union and help us to grow as a couple. We will not procrastinate, but we will use the foundational court values to guide us and steer us into living a peaceful relationship with one another.

Week 35

Love heals

There is nothing more powerful than love. It is, without doubt, God's healing agent for a broken heart. It is very seldom that you marry a completely whole person. So love is required to complete the healing process. The good news is that you get to enjoy the person you were instrumental in healing!

Tip

"Love never fails [never fades out or becomes obsolete or comes to an end]." (1 Corinthians 13:8 AMPC) This is a pretty powerful truth. If love never fails, then your marriage will not fail if you both walk in the love of God that has been shed abroad in your heart by the Holy Spirit (Romans 5:8). This also implies the power to heal marriage issues, because if love never fails, then it must have in it the ability to heal or correct what is wrong in a marriage. Yield to his love in your heart today. This is greater than romantic love, which is a must for a good marriage but cannot be the sustaining power of your marriage. Only *agape,* or the God kind of love, can heal, restore and re-fire your relationship.

Scripture

No one has ever seen God; but if we love one another,

God lives in us and his love is made complete in us. (1 John 4:12 NIV)

Exercise

Listen to the needs of your spouse. Listen through the love of God, shed abroad in your heart by the Holy Spirit. Love does not mean you turn a blind eye to problems and issues. Love does not mean you lay your head on a train track to be run over and crushed. Love means that you do what is necessary to resolve issues, to minister to your spouse, to care for them and believe that they can win! So love is forbearing, forgiving. Love can restore, revive, re-fire, redeem and rebuild anything in your relationship that is destroyed. Love never fails and therefore love never throws in the towel.

Live in love by the power of the Holy Spirit and turn the Holy Spirit loose in your relationship. When you yield to God's love in you, you will be the *first* beneficiary of your decision to follow after God in how you operate in the most important human relationship you will ever have. Minister to your spouse's needs as the Holy Spirit leads you. Ask that he help you be sensitive to their needs and be creative and Spirit-led in finding solutions together. God lives in you; you have the answers you need inside. Only believe, and move forward together.

Affirmation

We practice confessing the love scriptures regularly. We concentrate and focus on our weakest area so that we can be strengthened, not allowing it to become a hindrance in our relationship. God is love, and as people of God we will set an example of the Father God. Love is patient and kind. We are patient and kind to each other. We forgive one another at the beginning of the day, so when any offense occurs, we have already forgiven each other. We practice being slow to speak, slow to wrath and quick to hear. We ask our spouse for clarity before we respond. Our love heals, and there isn't anything greater than operating in the love of God to build and heal. We release *agape*, the God kind of love, in our marriage to heal, restore and re-fire our relationship.

Prayer

"Give thanks to the Lord, for he is good. His love endures forever. Give thanks to the God of gods. His love endures forever." (Psalm 136:1-2 NIV) Father, You are the God who is full of love, compassion and tender mercies. We will follow your example by walking in love and forgiveness towards one another. We will meditate throughout the day on 1 Corinthians 13:4-8 – *"Love endures with patience and serenity, love is kind and thoughtful, and is not jealous or envious; love does not brag and is not proud or arrogant. It is not rude; it is not self-seeking, it is not provoked [nor overly sensitive and easily angered]; it does not take into account a wrong endured. It does not rejoice at injustice, but rejoices with the truth [when right and truth prevail]. Love bears all*

things [regardless of what comes], believes all things [looking for the best in each one], hopes all things [remaining steadfast during difficult times], endures all things [without weakening]. Love never fails [it never fades nor ends]." (AMPC) Father, renew our love for each other every day.

A Marriage Investment Story . . .

No job and no money

I don't think there is anything worse for a man than to lose his job as the breadwinner. I remember how I felt when my boss told me he was going to have to let me go. My heart sank and I left my job pretty depressed. I went home and sat in the car for a minute to collect my thoughts. I went in and told Sandra I got laid off. The thing about Sandra is she grew up poor, and her mom taught her how to survive and make the best of her situation. Rhea was 13. Tasha was 6, Alexus was 3. So I was a little scared about not being able to support my family. We had some savings but not much. I started looking for another job immediately. Sandra and I spent two hours in the morning every day in prayer. Each day we went before the Lord about our needs and asking that he would lead me where to look for a job. This went on about two months. Each day we would get up early and pray for two hours, seeking the Lord for help. After this season I got a call back from one of my bosses who had laid me off. He said his partner was killed in a plane crash. The other technician demanded half of the company or he was going to walk. Tom asked me if I would consider coming back to work, because he had fired the other guy. Tom needed a technician immediately to handle maintenance accounts and help with installations for new sales. The great thing about this situation was he needed me to keep his income flowing. So Sandra and I prayed about what to do. The Lord spoke to our hearts that we were to take the job but ask for $1,000 back pay and twice as much salary as before. I received a word from the Lord that he had "commanded the ravens to feed me" (1 Kings 17:4) just as God supernaturally took care of Elijah through the ravens, giving him bread and flesh in the morning and evening. God would take care of me with this unsaved man of the world (raven). The Lord did exactly what he said, and Tom later received Jesus. I learned from my previous situation to pray for my boss in order to keep my life peaceful.

"First of all, then, I admonish and urge that petitions, prayers, intercessions, and thanksgivings be offered on behalf of all men,

"For kings and all who are in positions of authority or high responsibility, that [outwardly] we may pass a quiet and undisturbed life [and inwardly] a peaceable one in all godliness and reverence and seriousness in every way.

"For such [praying] is good and right, and [it is] pleasing and acceptable to God our Savior,

"Who wishes all men to be saved and [increasingly] to perceive and recognize and discern and know precisely and correctly the [divine] Truth." (1 Timothy 2:1-4 AMPC)

We believe people have a lot of unnecessary mishaps in their lives because they don't pray for the people that have the power to disturb their peace. **Proactive prayers are much more powerful than reactive prayers.**

It was the prayer of agreement with Sandra that moved the hand of God.

Week 36

Blended Families

The so-called "blended family" is no longer an aberration in American society: It's a norm. It has become the norm due to an increase in the number of children born outside the marriage union and an increase in divorce and remarriage. Since societal norms are in a constant state of flux, dealing with these complex issues is like trying to hit a moving target.

Tip

Blended families face four basic challenges:

1. Sibling Rivalry
2. Everyone Needs Attention
3. Stepparent Discipline Can Be a Challenge
4. You Feel Like Two Separate Families

God's love is *always* the default in dealing with issues and finding a solution. But what does the love of God look like in a blended family? You will have to spend time communicating the vision for this new arrangement. Why are you together and what do you desire to accomplish? This conversation must go beyond, "Mom and Dad just love each other, and you kids will just have to deal with it!" As a couple you must come into agreement about responsibility, discipline, handling conflict. You will also need to address fears you may have because of previous relationships. The key here is to agree *before* you "go public." If you find yourself caught into a public disagreement, pause and leave the situation, *privately* deal with the issues, and then share your solution with your children. Seek the Lord in how to address the main issues, and seek help for things beyond your ability to resolve. Most of all, don't *ignore* issues; that's like going the wrong way down a one-way street, full speed with your eyes closed. You are going to crash, and it might be fatal! Lastly, if you know your children have experienced some sexual assault or incest, communicate this to your spouse and prayerfully address the issues. In these cases, it is a high probability that sexual dysfunction can compound your new union challenges.

Scripture

Do to others as you would like them to do to you. (Luke 6:31)

Make allowance for each other's faults and forgive anyone who offends you. Remember, the Lord forgave you, so you must forgive others. Above all, clothe yourselves with love, which binds us all together in perfect harmony. And let the peace that comes from Christ rule in your hearts. For as members of one body you are called to live in peace. And always be thankful. (Colossians 3:13-16)

Exercise

Pray for the unity of your family three times this week.

Bring all of your children together and read the above scripture and discuss together what this looks like. Think of an activity you can do together; use this to develop a team spirit of unity and cooperation. Have your children pray for each other's needs. Meet monthly to discuss issues and find solutions *together*.

Affirmation

Father God, thank you that we operate in the love of God concerning our blended family. We use wisdom and love to deal with sibling rivalry, attention seeking, discipline, and the feeling of being two separate families. We are operating in the God kind of love, which creates the God kind of family. We love and treat our children from previous relationships as if they are our own children. We don't show partiality with any one of our children, but we treat all of our children equally. We are in agreement when it comes to how to raise our children. We make allowance for each other's faults, and forgive anyone who offends us. We pray for the unity of our family. We bring our children together and pray together to grow together as a family. We meet monthly to discuss issues and find solutions *together*.

Prayer

Father God, thank you for sending Jesus to the earth to destroy the works of the devil in our life. We ask your blessing on our family, the blessing of unity, love, patience. We thank you for the power to resolve any and all differences in Jesus' name. Deliver our family from every hindrance and work of darkness. Bind us together in perfect harmony, help us to walk in peace, and let the love and compassion of Jesus Christ rule in our hearts, in Jesus' name.

Week 37

Spiritual warfare

Spiritual warfare is real. As God *hates* divorce, the devil hates Christian marriages. Why? Because your presence in the world system is the greatest witness that Jesus is Lord!

Tip

When you encounter a conflict, understand that there is a *third party* present to pour gasoline on the fire that he most likely started! So, don't get caught up in the emotions of the moment; always realize that there is an evil intent behind every issue. This is not to say that the "devil made you do it," because we must all take responsibility for our behavior. But the more accurate statement is *the devil will help you do it and make it a lot worse!* So don't be naive. Since our battle is not with flesh and blood (each other, etc.), our response—not reaction—must be with the use of spiritual weaponry, such as applying the sword of the Spirit, which is the Word of God. This is not to be used on each other! But using the Word to address the issue at hand is the key to victory. This spiritual weaponry must also include praying in the Spirit, since we need the Holy Spirit to help us in what to pray for. *"And the Holy Spirit helps us in our weakness. For example, we don't know what God wants us to pray for. But the Holy Spirit prays for us with groanings that cannot be expressed in words. And the Father who knows all hearts knows what the Spirit is saying, for the Spirit pleads for us believers in harmony with God's own will." (Romans 8:26-27 NLT)* With the help of the Helper you can pray effectively and efficiently so that your prayers are not hindered, and you get results. Lastly, when you encounter a problem, address it swiftly and don't carry it over to the next day. Remember, all matters are resolved in 24 hours. Otherwise, unforgiveness will settle in your relationship and all of your faith and prayer will be neutralized through breaking the commandment of love.

Scripture

For though we walk in the flesh, we are not waging war according to the flesh. For the weapons of our warfare are not of the flesh but have divine power to destroy strongholds. We destroy arguments and every lofty opinion raised against the knowledge of God, and take every thought captive to obey Christ. (2 Corinthians 10:3-5 ESV)

Finally, be strong in the Lord and the strength of his might. Put on the whole armor of God, that you may be able to stand against the schemes of the devil. For we do not wrestle against flesh and blood, but against the rulers, against the authorities, against the cosmic powers over this present darkness, against the spiritual forces of evil in the heavenly places. (Ephesians 6:10-12 ESV)

Exercise

Look at the toughest issue you are facing in your relationship, and find scripture that promises you the victory. Focus your prayer and your faith on the issue. Use this scripture to praise the Lord for the answer. Lastly, when you encounter a conflict, stop and realize that the enemy has intent behind this issue; seek to pursue and establish the will of God in the midst of the issue. *"Your kingdom come, your will be done, on earth as it is in heaven." (Matthew 6:10)*

Affirmation

Greater is he that is in us than he that is in the world. If God be for us, who can be against us? We are strong in the Lord and the power of his might, and we put on the whole armor of God that we may be able to stand, having done all to stand. We stand against the enemy, the devil. We pray and meditate on these verses – *"Finally, be strong in the Lord and in the strength of his might. Put on the whole armor of God, that you may be able to stand against the schemes of the devil. For we do not wrestle against flesh and blood, but against the rulers, against the authorities, against the cosmic powers over this present darkness, against the spiritual forces of evil in the heavenly places." (Ephesians 6:10-12)* We bind up the powers of darkness operating over our life. We say we have victory in our marriage.

When we encounter conflict, we understand that there is a third party present to pour gasoline on the fire that he most likely started! We say to the third party, "Get out of our marriage in Jesus' name." We say we don't react to outbursts of anger but we respond in love. We say we will not operate on emotions and open the door to the enemy.

Prayer

Thank you, Father God, that you are our refuge and help in a time of need – *"But the Lord is faithful, and he will strengthen you and protect you from the evil one." (2 Thessalonians 3:3 NIV)*

We put our trust in you. We understand spiritual warfare is real; as you hate divorce, the devil hates Christian marriages. Though Satan goes around like a roaring lion seeking whom he may devour, we will not fear any attack, because we have "The Greater One" living inside of us. There is nothing to fear. We pray Isaiah 41:10, *"So do not fear for I am with you; do not be dismayed, for I am your God. I will strengthen you and help you; I will uphold you with my righteous right hand." (NIV)* We will stand against the attacks of the enemy and nothing by any means will harm us. We will put on the whole armor of God and stand against the evil one. We pray Ephesians 6:10-12 – *"Finally, be strong in the Lord and in the strength of his might. Put on the whole armor of God, that you may be able to stand against the schemes of the devil. For we do not wrestle against flesh and blood, but against the rulers, against the authorities, against the cosmic powers over this present darkness, against the spiritual forces of evil in the heavenly places." (ESV)* Jesus, you have given us authority, and we use our authority over all the works of the enemy in Jesus' name, amen.

Week 38

Fasting and prayer

When the disciples of Jesus failed to exorcise a very powerful demon, Jesus taught them, "This kind would only obey through prayer and fasting." On occasion, you will encounter this kind in the form of attack against your relationship and your family. Fasting and prayer is the only way to get results. Fasting and prayer is a powerful tool for couples to use in the midst of a firefight.

Tip

(Read Matthew 17:19-21 below in scripture section.)

The enemy hates to see a successful Christ-centered marriage. If the devil can destroy your marriage, this is one way he can extinguish the light of Jesus to a lost world. So it is in the devil's best interest to attack your marriage and destroy it completely. The enemy will send spiritual assassins against you more powerful than demons previously encountered. When this happens, you have to step up your game through fasting and prayer. Fasting and prayer are powerful on their own, but nothing—I mean absolutely nothing—is more powerful than when a husband and wife come together to fast and pray about an obstacle. You have the power of agreement at work, *and* you have the added power of fasting and prayer! When should you do this? The Holy Spirit will let you know when it is time to increase your power. According to scripture, you need to walk away from the food table and sex so that you can focus. (See 1 Corinthians 7:5 below.)

Scripture

*Then the disciples came to Jesus privately and said, "Why could we not cast it out?" So Jesus said to them, "Because of your unbelief; for assuredly, I say to you, if you have faith as a mustard seed, you will say to this mountain, 'Move from here to there,' and it will move, and nothing will be impossible for you. However, **this kind** does not go out except by prayer and fasting." (Matthew 17: 19-21 NKJV, emphasis added)*

*Do not deprive one another except with consent for a time, that you may give yourselves **to fasting and prayer**; and come together again so that Satan does not tempt you because of your lack of self-control. (1 Corinthians 7:5 NKJV, emphasis added)*

Exercise

Have a conversation about an area of your life where you have not been able to see a breakthrough. Write down the obstacle using the following steps:

1. What is the obstacle?
2. How long has this been troubling you?
3. What have you done about it so far?
4. Have you seen any results?
5. Why do you want to see a change in this area?
6. How will this breakthrough glorify God?
7. When is the best date and time to fast and pray without distractions?

8. What type of fast will you employ?
9. What are the start and stop dates?

Now that you have answered the questions, let's get going!

Affirmation

Jesus has given us the authority to cast out devils and over all the power of the enemy, and nothing by any means will hurt us. We will set aside time to fast and pray. When we recognize strongholds in our life that are not broken, we will take time to fast and pray as a couple. We spend quality time in agreement fasting and praying, because this is the is the only way to get results. God has given us this powerful tool of fasting and prayer as a couple in the midst of a firefight.

We stay strong as a Christian couple through fasting and praying. We fast and pray because we know the enemy hates to see a successful Christ-centered marriage.

We take time to write down areas that we need to fast and pray over, to break the power of the devil from our marriage.

We have a conversation about an area of our life that has not been able to see a breakthrough. We write down the obstacle, how long, what it is, etc. When we fast as a couple, we discuss how long we will be on our fast. We will observe this scripture – *"Do not deprive one another except with consent for a time, that you may give yourselves to* ***fasting and prayer****; and come together again so that Satan does not tempt you because of your lack of self-control." (1 Corinthians 7:5 NKJV, emphasis added)*

Prayer

Father, we worship and praise your magnificent name. We thank you for a powerful tool of fasting and prayer. Jesus taught his disciples to fast and pray in Matthew17:19-21 – *"Then the disciples came to Jesus privately and said, 'Why could we not cast it out?' So Jesus said to them, 'Because of your unbelief; for assuredly, I say to you, if you have faith as a mustard seed, you will say to this mountain, "Move from here to there," and it will move, and nothing will be impossible for you. However,* ***this kind*** *does not go out except by prayer and fasting.'" (NKJV, emphasis added)* There will be times in our marriage where we will have difficulty in resolving conflict or attacks of the enemy. But your Word says this kind comes out by prayer and fasting. Lord Jesus, we will use your example, and we will fast and pray and break the power of the enemy from our marriage. We declare we have the authority to break the power of the devil. So our prayer to you today, Father, has strengthened us with the power of your Holy Spirit. Speak to us in times of fasting and prayer so we will be strengthened with might by the power of the Holy Spirit. You have given us all the things about life and godliness. We will use our times of fasting and prayer to come closer to you and to be strengthened and free from all the works of the enemy.

Week 39

Emotional disorder

Emotional disorder is a very broad term, and many disorders can fall under two major headings: Mood and Anxiety disorders.

Mood disorders are characterized by a mood or emotions that are not appropriate to a given situation.

Anxiety disorders occur when an individual remains in a persistent state of anxiety for an extended period of time.

These two types of disorders are also broad categories that contain more specific disorders under their respective umbrellas.

The point is in marriage some of the issues you may be facing may be attributed to some type of disorder, and you will need both spiritual and medical (in some cases legal) help to work through these. In some cases, your spouse may not be willing to do what is necessary to improve this area of his/her life. In that case you will need to seek outside counsel beyond this devotional to know what to do moving forward.

Tip

Emotional disorders are alive and well in relationships today. The problem is many people are in denial about this. In some communities to suggest your spouse may be dealing with an emotional disorder can cause a fight! *I ain't crazy!!!* However, there is nothing CRAZY about acknowledging your need for help if you have experienced some type of trauma or are dealing with a chemical imbalance, etc. You owe it to yourself and your family to get the help you need. Address your pride and look at the larger picture. You cannot expect your spouse to suffer in this relationship if you are unwilling to address real issues that are beyond your control due to a disorder. Take responsibility to love yourself, your spouse and your children and do something about your situation. Do it now.

Scripture

The Spirit of the Lord [is] upon Me, because He has anointed Me [the Anointed One, the Messiah] to preach the good news (the Gospel) to the poor; He has sent Me to announce release to the captives and recovery of sight to the blind, to send forth as delivered those who are oppressed [who are downtrodden, bruised, crushed, and broken down by calamity], to proclaim the accepted and acceptable year of the Lord [the day when salvation and the free favors of God profusely abound.] (Luke 4:18-19 AMPC)

Exercise

Take an inventory of your behavior over a period of time. Look for frequency, such as recurrence during certain times of the year. Look for words, attitudes and actions that trigger irregular and uncharacteristic behaviors. Search online about symptoms of emotional disorders. Be prayerful about this sensitive area and ask the Holy Spirit to help you both to work through this issue if you see patterns and symptoms. If you are dealing with an emotional disorder, your spouse is the best support you will ever have. Talk about it, pray about it and take action.

Affirmation

We take an inventory of our behavior over a period of time. We look for frequency, such as recurrence during certain times of the year. We look for words, attitudes and actions that trigger irregular and uncharacteristic behaviors. We are open and honest with each other, and it is important to us that we address issues that potentially are damaging to our relationship. We search online about symptoms of emotional disorders. We are not fearful when God gives us the courage to follow through without anger and rebuttal with one another. We are prayerful about this sensitive area and ask the Holy Spirit to help us both work through this issue if we see patterns and symptoms. We believe Jesus is the same yesterday today and forever, and he is here with us today, healing us of all emotional disorders, mood disorders and anxiety disorders. Thank you, Jesus, for your anointing to set us free.

Prayer

Father, we adore and worship your holy name; you are a wonderful God, everlasting and Prince of Peace. Father, you sent Jesus your Son here on the earth to deliver us from the works of the devil. Lord we receive who you are in our lives and marriage according to Luke 4:18-19 – *"The Spirit of the Lord [is] upon Jesus, because the Father has anointed Jesus [the Anointed One, the Messiah] to preach the good news to us; the Father has sent Jesus to announce our release from all captivity and recovery of sight so that we have clarity and direction. Jesus was sent forth to deliver us from oppression [downtrodden, bruised, crushed, and broken down by calamity]. Jesus was sent to proclaim the accepted and acceptable year of the Lord to us so that we may* ***recover all!*** *[the day when salvation and the free favors of God profusely abound] upon our marriage and family." (AMPC, adapted)* Jesus, you are anointed to heal and deliver us from emotional disorders, trauma and every name that is named. Restore our mind and emotions back to complete health. In Jesus' name!

Week 40

Health and wellness

Being physically fit and eating healthy enhance the quality of life in marriage.

Tip

It is important that you commit as a couple to pursue a healthy lifestyle. Proper eating, sufficient water and a consistent age-appropriate workout plan are absolute musts to building a high-quality relationship. We know all the excuses! Our children, our job, ministry, career and business pursuits—we just don't have the time. Here is the thing: You *will* have the time when something breaks down or when your life is threatened. So be proactive and get a fitness coach or start something as simple as walking a few evenings or mornings per week. *Do something!* And be consistent. Rethink eating out; limit this both for your budget and more importantly for the health risks of eating restaurant food too often—especially fast food. It's really bad for your overall health. Drink more water; you know the drill. Just do it! By the way, with more energy and a slimmer look, your sex life will be awesome!

Scripture

Do you not know that in a race all the runners run, but only one receives the prize? So run that you may obtain it.

Every athlete exercises self-control in all things. They do it to receive a perishable wreath, but we an imperishable. So I do not run aimlessly; I do not box as one beating the air. But I discipline my body and keep it under control, lest after preaching to others I myself should be disqualified. (1 Corinthians 9:24-27 ESV)

Exercise

- Ask the Holy Spirit to help you in this area of your life.
- Sit down for a minute and talk about *why* you need to commit to a health and wellness *plan*.
- Measure your weight, your inches and keep a log. (Don't be afraid, you have to start somewhere.)
- Take inventory on how much you are spending eating out.
- Keep a diary this week on *everything you stuff in your face*. We mean for real. Compare notes with each other and talk about it.
- Next, set a very small incremental plan to cut back on what and how much you are eating.
- Add more fruit and vegetables and cut back on late-night eating.
- Consider having your larger meals during the day and smaller meals at night.
- Get a really nice water bottle and drink approximately one-half your current body weight in ounces.
- Determine how many times you need to fill it up to meet your water goal.

- Consider cutting back on bread and sweets.
- Think about working out *together* (great quality time). If you can't do it each workout, commit to at least once per week.
- Go to www.fitnessblender.com. You can find workout plans, meal plans, and a host of tips. We like that a husband and wife are the founders. Check it out!
- Set a collective goal, total inches and pounds, and *go for it!*
- Share your plan with another couple in your life and ask them to hold you accountable.

Affirmation

Being physically fit and eating healthy enhances the quality of life in marriage. We commit as a couple to pursue a healthy lifestyle. We have proper eating habits, we drink sufficient water, and we have a consistent age-appropriate workout plan. We are building a high-quality relationship. We will not use excuses like our children, our job, ministry, career, and business pursuits or "we just don't have the time." We take advantage of walking or running in our neighborhood. We are proactive, and we have a coach; we will make a commitment as a couple to pursue a healthy lifestyle. We will not wait for our bodies to break down before we engage in a healthy lifestyle. *We will do something now!* And be consistent. We are healthy, active and living to be the future "Centennials."

Prayer

Father God, help us to be proactive in living a healthy lifestyle. We desire to live until we are Centennials. Father, give us the discipline and desire to run this race and win. We need your help to see it through to the end and finish what you have asked us to do. We ask the Holy Spirit to help us in this area of our life. We submit our thoughts and plans concerning being healthy and proactive. We know it is not by might nor by power but by your Spirit. Holy Spirit, you are the great creator; create in us a desire, discipline, and delight for being fit, fabulous and strong. We ask that you would lead us so we will not run aimlessly. Our prayer is to exercise self-control in all things as we discipline our bodies and keep them under control with the fruit of temperance.

A Marriage Investment Story…

Why did you talk to me like that?

Sandra and I got into a little spat over some issue. I said something really mean and cruel to her, just short of cursing her out. I walked away from her with a little "I am the man walk." The Holy Spirit stopped me in my tracks and asked me a question. "Why did you talk to me like that?"

I was startled! "I wasn't talking to you, Holy Spirit, I was talking to her!"

"Did not my Word say:"

"Now as he went on his way, he approached Damascus, and suddenly a light from heaven shone around him. And falling to the ground, he heard a voice saying to him, 'Saul, Saul, why are you persecuting me?' And he said, 'Who are you, Lord?' And he said, 'I am Jesus, whom you are persecuting. But rise and enter the city, and you will be told what you are to do.'" (Acts 9:3-6 ESV)

"Paul had never seen Jesus, and yet what he did to Christians, he was doing to Jesus!"

Then the Spirit said, "And what about my Word in Matthew?"

"'For I was hungry, and you gave me food, I was thirsty, and you gave me drink, I was a stranger, and

you welcomed me, I was naked, and you clothed me, I was sick, and you visited me, I was in prison, and you came to me.' Then the righteous will answer him, saying, 'Lord, when did we see you hungry and feed you, or thirsty and give you drink? And when did we see you a stranger and welcome you, or naked and clothe you? And when did we see you sick or in prison and visit you?' And the King will answer them, **'Truly, I say to you, as you did it to one of the least of these my brothers, you did it to me.'** *'Then he will say to those on his left, "Depart from me, you cursed, into the eternal fire prepared for the devil and his angels. For I was hungry, and you gave me no food, I was thirsty, and you gave me no drink, I was a stranger, and you did not welcome me, naked, and you did not clothe me, sick and in prison, and you did not visit me." Then they also will answer, saying, 'Lord, when did we see you hungry or thirsty or a stranger or naked or sick or in prison, and did not minister to you?' Then he will answer them, saying,* **'Truly, I say to you, as you did not do it to one of the least of these, you did not do it to me.'"** *(Matthew 25:35-45 ESV, emphasis added)*

"So even if you consider your wife to be least, what you do to her you do to me. Now I ask you again, why did you talk to me like that?"

I was speechless; not only did I insult and hurt Sandra, but I just ticked off the Holy Spirit! Not good! So, I turned around immediately and apologized to

Sandra. "I am sorry, Sandra; will you forgive me for what I said?" She did and we kissed and made up. I learned a very valuable lesson. What I did to Sandra I was doing to Jesus, so I had better treat her good!

Week 41

Past Hurts

Past hurts can impact your future.

Tip

Past hurts in your life, can have a drastic impact on your marriage. These include hurts growing up, hurts from previous relationships and hurts in your current relationship. If you don't let go of the past, you won't have a future. Getting a new spouse won't cure you. Why? Because when you start the new relationship, *you* are in it. This includes all of your baggage. So what do you do? Let go, forgive, release, move on. "Well, if it were that easy, I would have done that *already*!" You cannot do things in the flesh. Remember what Jesus said – *"I am the vine; you are the branches. Whoever abides in me and I in him, he it is that bears much fruit, for apart from me you can do nothing." (John 15:5)* So let's do it right. Ask the Holy Spirit to show you the *path to your healing*. He will!

Scripture

The Lord is my shepherd; I shall not want. He makes me lie down in green pastures. He leads me beside still waters. ***He restores my soul.*** *He leads me in paths of righteousness for his name's sake. (Psalm 23:1-3 ESV, emphasis added)*

Exercise

When you encounter a conflict or get irritated about a recent encounter, ask yourself: "How much of this is about what just happened or is this a buildup of past issues, fears, resentment, bitterness, etc.?" When you explode or implode, it is usually a result of an unresolved issue in the past. We also tell couples if you have been in a bad relationship before, you will punish your current spouse for what the other person did to you for a season. An example: If you were in a marriage or relationship for, say, five years, it generally takes three to five years to overcome the effects of the negative relationship. So, our counsel is to be patient with your spouse; they don't realize they are punishing you for the other jerk's jack-legged behavior!

If the hurt is a result of your current relationship, if you have not addressed the issue, you need to do so now. Letting it continue will only erode your relationship. When you bury an issue, you are not really burying it; you are actually *planting* it! So now it will grow *roots of bitterness. "Try to be at peace with everyone, and try to live a holy life, because no one will see the Lord without it. Guard against turning back from the grace of God. Let no one become like a bitter plant that grows up and causes many troubles with its poison." (Hebrews 12:14-15 GNT)* As found in scripture, roots of bitterness will defile your relationship. So you must prayerfully talk things out, forgive and don't bring up the past again. If you are really struggling, you may need to get help. Address it quickly.

Affirmation

We will walk in love and keep our heart pure and free from the buildup of past hurts. Past hurts in our life will not have a drastic impact on our marriage. We apply the principles of love and forgiveness every time there is an issue. We release all past issues and trauma we experienced before marriage. We release any residue of issues buried in our heart from traumatic offenses, rape, molestation, abuse and fears. We release all hurts growing up, hurts in previous relationships and hurts in our current relationship. We let go of the past! Past hurts, you won't have a future in our life. We decree and let go, we forgive, release, move on. We remember what Jesus said in John 15:5, *"I am the vine; you are the branches. Whoever abides in me and I in him, he it is that bears much fruit, for apart from me you can do nothing." (ESV)* We will do it right; we ask the Holy Spirit to show us the *path to our healing*.

Prayer

Lord Jesus, you are my Shepherd, and I shall not want. Receive my prayer today – *"The Lord is my shepherd; I shall not want. He makes me lie down in green pastures. He leads me beside still waters. He restores my soul. He leads me (us) in paths of righteousness for his name's sake." (Psalm 23:1-3 ESV)* Father God, anoint our heads with oil and renew in us hearts free from the impact of all traumatic experiences. Give us the grace and understanding to work through all current grievous hurts from one another. Refresh our minds and hearts about how much we loved each other before the damage in our relationship. Fast forward us to a place of peaceful resting places. Let us not stew and harp over what we did to each other, but instead to welcome your love and sovereignty of the Holy Spirit, our helper. Teach us to love and forgive like our Lord and Savior Jesus Christ.

Week 42

Pornography

Pornography is a very serious issue today, and it is getting worse, even amongst the Lord's people. Josh McDowell says, "Porn is probably the greatest threat to the church in its existence." Pornography use has become less taboo among Americans, appeals to both men and women and is prevalent among Christians and non-Christians alike. But the number of Christians viewing pornography virtually mirrors the national average.

Tip

Barna's editor-in-chief, Roxanne Stone, notes, "The most common definition of pornography among Americans is any image used for sexual arousal or masturbation." Porn is not just a "male matter" anymore. Roughly 55 to 70 percent of men and 30 to 40 percent of women under age 40 reported viewing pornography in a given year.

An article from *Married a* shares their research on the "Effects of pornography on Marriage." Exposure to porn produces the following:

- Marital Dissatisfaction
- Negative and damaging Impact on Wives
- Emotional Separation (dissatisfaction with, and even distaste for, a spouse's affection.)

- Increased Infidelity
- Separation and Divorce

If porn has found its way in your marriage, what do you do? Prayer is always the start. Next, talk with a trusted, mature in Christ friend if you don't feel you are ready to talk about it as a couple. Porn addiction can result from previous sexual behavior, demonic influence in a person's life, abuses and sexual violations, such as incest and rape. So don't rush to the conclusion that your spouse's porn addiction is your fault. Speaking to wives here, some women have reported that they have sex with their husband multiple times per week, and even per day, and *still he is doing porn!* So obviously the problem is beyond his need for sex from his wife. However, we have witnessed many cases where the wife is available for sex only once per month or, sometimes months—even years! Deal with the problem head-on and take small steps to heal your marriage. God, your heavenly Father, wants you to be addicted to each other and not to a sleazy, filthy Moabitish reprobate!

Scripture

I will set nothing wicked before my eyes; I hate the work of those who fall away; it shall not cling to me. (Psalm 101:3 NKJV)

Exercise

Have a conversation about sexual intimacy in your marriage. On a scale from one to ten, ask your spouse to give you a number. This is for both of you. If they have a low number, ask what is the reason for that number? Listen carefully and empathize with them.

Next, have a conversation about porn and masturbation. This can be a difficult conversation to have. Only engage if you are ready to hear the truth without exploding or having a meltdown. If you suspect an issue, and you don't feel you can handle things properly, you may want to get outside help. You have to know yourself and your spouse before you try this.

If you are dealing with porn, determine the steps to be open and honest with your spouse. You may want to have a conversation with someone first. If your spouse confesses that they are doing porn, it is hard not to feel betrayed, angry and worthless in your relationship. Be aware that if your spouse confesses to you about porn, that has taken a great deal of courage to do so. Know that they truly love you and desire to be free. Remember, the love of God has been shed abroad in your heart, so you can minister to them and love them through this trial. Lastly, be encouraged and know that the Lord has your relationship in his hands. He is guiding you and will bring you to a higher landing place. (1 Corinthians 10:13)

Affirmation

We are free from pornography in our marriage. When one of us is tempted to watch porn, the other one is ready to bring support, pray and stand together to help get the victory in this area. We ask God to guide us and strengthen us from getting caught up in the trap of pornography.

Together we stand against the spirits of the lust of the flesh and the lust of the eyes. We will not engage in pornography, gross "funny" TV shows, movies and the like. We will be alerted by the Holy Spirit, our helper.

Prayer

Father, we lift up the name of Jesus today, for the name of Jesus is greater than any name. At the name of Jesus, every knee shall bow, and every tongue shall confess that Jesus is Lord. Father God, Jesus came to loosen and set us free from the power of the devil. Satan comes to kill, steal and destroy, but you have come that we might have life and have it more abundantly. We ask that you keep us loving you and each other more and more. Place in us your agape love and lead us into the path of righteousness. Pornography is the work of the devil. It comes to steal our satisfaction from one another. Lord Jesus, we repent for operating in lust and allowing our flesh to be in control. We ask that through the power of the Holy Spirit that you set us free from pornography. Lord, keep us free from this deadly sexual menace that destroys every marriage. We will set nothing wicked before our eyes.

Week 43

Secret sauce to marriage, part 1 (Educate your mind)

Most people don't have everything they need to be successful in marriage. If they did, we would not see such a high rate of divorce. You can only live out the pictures you embrace. The Secret Sauce to marriage starts with educating your mind.

Tip

Building a successful marriage requires learning and acquiring a new set of skills: Communication, conflict resolution, emotional intelligence, compromise, self-control, temperament, personality traits and stress management. All of these words represent a host of skills you will need to acquire if you are going to have a lifelong marriage. It is by no means a simple walk in the park. To be truthful, it is very hard to achieve success in this area. It takes a tremendous amount of energy, focus, persistence, forbearance, perseverance and tenacity. But it can be done if you want success badly enough. The first step is education and, for some, re-education. Read the Bible, read books on the subject, attend classes and workshops. The education process of marriage life is never-ending, and you will never learn enough nor learn it all. So, be teachable and commit to being a continual learner. In the end, the payback is almost unbelievable. There are no words to describe unending, seasoned love. When you grow together intellectually through learning, you paint new pictures that will shape who you are inside. The image you have of your marriage inside of your hearts will manifest for the world to see. You don't have to say anything about your marriage—people just see it and sense it. It is an amazing place to be!

Scripture

But the path of the [uncompromisingly] just and righteous is like the light of dawn, that shines more and more (brighter and clearer) until [it reaches its full strength and glory in] the perfect day [to be prepared]. (Proverbs 4:18 AMPC)

Exercise

Review our list of recommending reading. Commit to reading *together* one book each quarter—four books per year. Talk about what you are learning, and practice what you learn.

Affirmation

The Secret Sauce in our marriage is to educate our minds. God is giving us everything we need to have a successful marriage. We are creating successful pictures of marriage and renewing our mind to what it takes to have a successful, happy marriage. We will live out the positive pictures we embrace as we build upon our marriage union. To build our marriage, we are learning and acquiring a new set of skills. We are learning how to communicate, overcome conflict, develop in emotional intelligence, compromise, build on our self-control, understand each other's temperament, enjoy each other's personality traits and stress management. We are reaching towards the mark of the higher call in our marriage. God is leading us into the pathway of success. *"But the path of the [uncompromisingly] just and righteous is like the light of dawn, that shines more and more (brighter and clearer) until [it reaches its full strength and glory in] the perfect day [to be prepared]." (Proverbs 4:18 AMPC)*

Prayer

We worship you, the mighty God. We surrender leadership to you in our marriage. We delight in growing and developing in the Secret Sauce, educating our mind to be the best spouse we can be. Develop in our marriage wisdom in how to have a successful marriage. Father God, show us how to build a successful marriage as we acquire new sets of skills. Breathe on us with your holy breath of life to change our marriage from glory to glory. Father, increase our level of communication when we are discussing issues. Breathe on us so we will avoid and overcome conflict. Open our eyes so we can have a deeper understanding of emotional intelligence issues; teach us to compromise with one another. Lord, deliver us from temper tantrums and out-of-control behavior, and give us a new level of self-control. Father, with your help we will be able to learn each other's temperament and personality traits. Lord, help us to manage our stress. Together, as we grow, we will develop into a couple who has a lasting love for each other.

Week 44

Secret sauce to marriage, part 2 (Tenderize your heart)

There is nothing more important than your heart when it comes to cultivating a lifelong, loving relationship. Jesus said the only reason for divorce is the hardness of your heart. So it is vital that we have a tender heart in dealing with one another. That is to say, to show gentleness, concern and empathy.

Tip

"He said to them, Because of the hardness (stubbornness and perversity) of your hearts Moses permitted you to dismiss and repudiate and divorce your wives; but from the beginning, it has not been so [ordained]." (Matthew 19:8 AMPC).

Divorce as an option was never God's original design. In fact, the Bible says – *"'For I hate divorce!' says the Lord, the God of Israel. 'To divorce your wife is to overwhelm her with cruelty,' says the Lord of Heaven's Armies. 'So guard your heart; do not be unfaithful to your wife.'" (Malachi 2:16 NLT)* According to this verse, God hates divorce, because it is considered cruelty to one another. Notice the Lord says "guard" your heart. So divorce is a *heart* issue. Jesus used the term *hardness* of heart. This word *hardness* is translated "unyielding in behavior or attitude."

In other words, an unyielding person is saying, "*I will not* yield to God's Word, or the love of God shed abroad in my heart by the Holy Spirit (see Romans 5:8), nor will I yield to the gentle, loving and compassionate Holy Spirit, the heavenly dove who empowers me to fulfill the ministry of reconciliation. I *can* reconcile, *but I will not do it!*

So, with a tender heart or heart of flesh, you can build a vibrant love-filled marriage. The secret sauce to a successful marriage is to educate your mind and tenderize your heart. The word *tenderize* means to "make (meat or meat products) tender by applying a process or substance that breaks down connective tissue." *If* you are born again, you have a new heart and a new spirit. According to scripture, God has removed the heart of stone, and you now have a heart of flesh. So you now can be yielded and teachable. You have the capacity through Christ to be compassionate to each other and to show gentleness, concern and empathy just like the Holy Spirit who lives in you both. Yield to *him* today.

Scripture

He said to them, Because of the hardness (stubbornness and perversity) of your hearts Moses permitted you to dismiss and repudiate and divorce your wives; but from the beginning, it has not been so [ordained]. (Matthew 19:8 AMPC).

And I will give you a new heart, and a new spirit I will put within you. And I will remove the heart of stone from your flesh and give you a heart of flesh. And I will put my Spirit within you, and cause you to walk in my statutes and be careful to obey my rules. (Ezekiel 36: 26-27 ESV)

Exercise

Ask each other the following questions:

- Is there anything that I am currently doing that really bothers you, causes you pain or provokes you to "go off"?
- Why do you think my behavior makes you feel that way?
- What would you like me to do differently?

Without defending or justifying yourself through fault-finding, say: "I am sorry for causing you pain, hurt and frustration. Please forgive me. I will make the necessary adjustment to accommodate your request."

If there is something in your spouse's request that you feel is unreasonable, stay focused on the *issue* and provide a compromise so that you both are satisfied with the request. (The last thing that you want to do is to agree to something that you cannot fulfill or that you feel is unreasonable.) If you are not able to come to agreeable terms, providing you are both submitted to the Word, you may want to request a coaching session to work through the process of agreement.

Affirmation

The Secret Sauce in our marriage is to "Tenderize our heart." There is nothing more important than our heart when it comes to cultivating a lifelong, loving relationship. We are investing in marriage for a lifetime of love and happiness. We make sure that we have a *tender* heart in dealing with one another. We refuse to harden our hearts and create a breach in our marriage relationship. Jesus said in Matthew 19:8, *"...Because of the hardness (stubbornness and perversity) of your hearts Moses permitted you to dismiss and repudiate and divorce your wives; but from the beginning, it has not been so [ordained]."* (AMPC) We decided before marriage that divorce was not an option! God *hates* divorce because it is considered cruelty to one another. We vow never to be so cruel as to get a divorce because we did not keep our heart tenderized. We keep the power of love in our marriage by developing the Secret Sauce to a successful marriage, educating our mind and tenderizing our heart. Lord, create and purify our heart in areas where we have allowed it to harden.

Prayer

Father God, create in us a new heart and a new spirit. Remove all the stony callouses in our hearts that have built up from previous hurts. Today we wipe our hearts' slate clean and start fresh again. We will not allow our hearts to harden towards one another. Create in us a heart filled with lovingkindness and tender mercies for each other. We stand on Ezekiel 36:26-27, which says, *"And I will give you a new heart, and a new spirit I will put within you. And I will remove the heart of stone from your flesh and give you a heart of flesh. And I will put my Spirit within you, and cause you to walk in my statutes and be careful to obey my rules." (ESV)* Father God, open our eyes so we will be able to guard our hearts against hidden issues. Give us the capacity to yield to the Holy Spirit and each other. We will yield to each other always and never allow hurts to harden our hearts and make us to become unyielding. We submit ourselves to you. Father, direct our feet into the pathway of peace.

Week 45

Spiritual core training

Your spiritual life together is the root system of your marriage union. Spiritual core training is paramount in building your root system.

Tip

Core exercises include movements that activate a group of muscles called the core. These muscles work as a group to help stabilize and control the spine. Core exercise is exercise that focuses on the stabilization, endurance or strengthening of the core muscles. So when we use the term "spiritual core training" (SCT), we are talking about those spiritual activities that produce stabilization, endurance and strength in your spiritual being. Your spiritual being is the *core* of your existence. Your spiritual being is where the Holy Spirit dwells. Thus, spiritual core training maximizes your relationship with the Holy Spirit. It is the essential training that enables you to endure an attack on your relationship and come out as victors, promoted to a higher landing place.

We recall that in the movie *The Incredible Hulk*, attacking him only made him grow larger and stronger. Think about that for a moment. Every attack on our marriage, every obstacle standing in our way, will only make us bigger and stronger! Spiritual Core Training (SCT) will accomplish this every time. Like in all training, you never *stop* training.

SCT is a part of your lifestyle, not something you work in, but something that is a part of your life, just like breathing, eating and sleeping. As a couple, it is essential that you spend time in the Word and in prayer, set aside seasons of fasting and prayer, attend retreats, engage in fellowship with believers, study resources and be spiritual reproducers (soul-winning and discipleship) *together*. This is a non-negotiable. Not to do so will *weaken* your will to submit to God's Word and God's ways. The enemy will penetrate your hedge and wipe you out. He wants to put you on display as a defeated *so-called* Christian couple—NEVER!! Make SCT who you are and what you do as a God-designed couple.

Scripture

Blessed is the man
who walks not in the counsel of the wicked,
nor stands in the way of sinners,
nor sits in the seat of scoffers;
but his delight is in the law of the Lord,
and on his law he meditates day and night.
He is like a tree
planted by streams of water
that yields its fruit in its season,
and its leaf does not wither.
In all that he does, he prospers. (Psalm 1:1-3 ESV)

Exercise

Discuss the SCT activities highlighted below:

- Word
- Prayer
- Seasons of fasting and prayer
- Attend retreats
- Engage in fellowship with believers
- Study resources
- Spiritual reproducers

Develop and plan to work together to do your SCT.

Affirmation

We work together to develop a good *root system* in our marriage union Spiritual Core Training is paramount in building our root system, so we give special attention to root building and development. We spend quality time with our core exercise to bring stabilization, endurance and strengthening of the core areas of our marriage. We are using resources that help us in spiritual core root growth and development. We consistently read the Word daily. Prayer is key to our connection with God. We block out time for fasting and prayer. We spend time going to retreats to help us become more in tune with each other. We study resources to grow and overcome weakness. We are spiritual reproducers bringing others to Christ. We shall be like a tree planted by the rivers of water. *"Blessed is the man who walks not in the counsel of the wicked, nor stands in the way of sinners, nor sits in the seat of scoffers;*

but his delight is in the law of the Lord, and on his law he meditates day and night." (Psalm 1:1-2 ESV)

Prayer

Father God, we are so grateful to have you as our Lord and Savior. In Psalm 1:1-3 you say, *"Blessed is the man who walks not in the counsel of the wicked, nor stands in the way of sinners, nor sits in the seat of scoffers; but his delight is in the law of the Lord, and on his law he meditates day and night. He is like a tree planted by streams of water that yields its fruit in its season, and its leaf does not wither. In all that he does, he prospers." (ESV)* We work together to develop a good ROOT SYSTEM in our marriage union. Spiritual CORE TRAINING is the lifeline to building a foundation in our marriage and each other. Father, bless us as we pray, read the Word and have seasons of fasting and prayer. It is in you that we move and live and have our being.

Week 46

Boundaries

"Boundaries are anything that helps to differentiate you from someone else, or show where you begin and end." While the goal in marriage is to become one flesh, this does not mean either of you ceases to exist as an individual. It means that your union creates new dimensions of who you each are as a person and what you can both become together.

Tip

"And the rib that the Lord God had taken from the man he made into a woman and brought her to the man. Then the man said, 'This, at last, is bone of my bones and flesh of my flesh; she shall be called Woman because she was taken out of Man.' Therefore a man shall leave his father and his mother and hold fast to his wife, and they shall become one flesh." (Genesis 2:22-24 ESV) According to scripture, the goal in marriage is to "become one." For some couples, this means that you no longer exist as an individual, but your *purpose* is to be *whatever* your spouse needs you to be. This mindset can lead to a WIN/LOSE scenario. This would also mean you have no rights, no opinion, no contribution and you are essentially a *slave* to your spouse's needs, desires, wishes and whims! Lastly, this is what a co-dependent, toxic relationship looks like. We don't think God

would look at this type of relationship and say to himself, "Now this couple is *exactly* what I had in mind when I created the husband and wife!" Boundaries mean that you have the *freedom* to be who you are, and at the same time unite as a team to accomplish together what you could never accomplish individually.

Scripture

In [this] freedom Christ has made us free [and completely liberated us]; stand fast then, and do not be hampered and held ensnared and submitted again to a yoke of slavery [which you have once put off]. (Galatians 5:1 AMPC)

Exercise

Have a conversation with each other about the issue of "freedom and control." Ask the following questions:

- Is there anything I am doing that makes you feel like I am controlling you?
- What would you like me to do differently?

Take personal responsibility for your behavior and reflect on *why* you are controlling your spouse. Is it fear, past hurts, trauma or other issue—perhaps in your childhood or previous relationships?

Now reverse roles and ask the same questions.

Affirmation

We are committed to honor boundaries. Our goal in marriage is to become one flesh. This does not mean either of us ceases to exist as an individual. Our union creates new dimensions of who we are as a person and what we can both become together. God created woman from man, but this does not mean the woman only exists for her husband. *"And the rib that the Lord God had taken from the man he made into a woman and brought her to the man. Then the man said, 'This at last is bone of my bones and flesh of my flesh; she shall be called Woman, because she was taken out of Man.' Therefore a man shall leave his father and his mother and hold fast to his wife, and they shall become one flesh." (Genesis 2:22-24 ESV)* We will not cease to exist because we are becoming one flesh. We ensure in our marriage that we both have freedom without controls.

Prayer

Father, you are the great I AM, we worship your holy name. We are committed to grow together. We are free to be individuals, yet function as a team in the unity of the Spirit in the bond of peace. Father, help us serve one another in love and humility, never out of unreasonable expectations, control and demands. We worship you, for you always cause everything to work together for good in our marriage. We will set appropriate boundaries in our relationship, never expecting each other to be our slave. We will not take advantage of our spouse's weakness. We will strive to never harass, make them feel guilty, or bully one another and take each other for granted. In Jesus' name.

Week 47

Emotional intelligence? Really?

"It's about being smarter with feelings. More aware. More intentional. More purposeful."

Tip

Ever since Daniel Goleman wrote his book, *Emotional Intelligence* or EQ, there has been a flood of articles, workshops, lunch and learn sessions, books and video content on the subject. Why is this such a huge topic? It's because people are emotionally driven and can't seem to get beyond their emotions to resolve any real problems. Marriages are no different. With divorce rates so high, especially in second and third marriages, it is amazing that people still want to get married.

Emotional Intelligence is about knowing and managing your emotions, knowing and managing the emotions of others and creating an environment of synergy so you can get things done. If one person is emotionally intelligent, they would see drastic improvements in their marriage. But what would happen if both husband and wife were well trained and accomplished in Emotional Intelligence? We think heaven would come down and kiss the earth and they would get caught in the smack!

Scripture

But the fruit of the Spirit is love, joy, peace, patience, kindness, goodness, faithfulness, gentleness, self-control; against such things there is no law. (Galatians 5:22 ESV)

Exercise

Google "emotional intelligence" and read a few articles and view some content until you both can grasp the concepts. Also, visit our website and watch a video entitled "Christ-centered Emotional Intelligence":

www.MarriageEquitySystems.com

Lastly, take a quiz and learn the personality traits of each other by visiting

https://www.gotoquiz.com/personality_plus_1

Affirmation

We are growing and maturing in the area of Emotional Intelligence, because Emotional Intelligence is about being smarter with feelings and being more intentional and more purposeful." We purpose in our heart and actions to study materials on Emotional Intelligence so we will not "head bump" each other day in and day out. No, we are smarter than that, and we are committed to not operating as *"bone heads"* with an EQ of less than 10. We will grow and improve ourselves with Emotional Intelligence principles to lessen the chances of becoming a statistic of divorce. Emotional Intelligence is about knowing and managing our emotions, knowing and managing the emotions of others and creating an environment of synergy so we can get things done. We have a high EQ to manage our emotions, manage the emotions of others and create an environment of synergy so we can get things done.

Prayer

Father, we acknowledge that you are Lord of this entire universe. We receive you as Master, Savior and Prince of Peace. Overshadow us with your power and love. Allow your anointing to fall on our marriage every day. Infuse us with your love and cause us to walk in wisdom. Deepen our understanding of how to grow in Emotional Intelligence. We recognize that no human being is more emotionally intelligent than the Holy Spirit. He produces the fruit of the Spirit, which are love, joy, peace, patience, kindness, goodness, faithfulness, gentleness and self-control. Walking in the Spirit and thereby producing the fruit of the Spirit is the most emotionally intelligent we could ever be! Help us, Lord, to mature so that we may glorify you in our sacred union.

Week 48

Abuse

"Twenty people are abused by an intimate partner every minute in the United States." "Seventy percent of domestic violence related murders happen when the victim tries to leave their abuser." Abuse is a difficult area to discuss. However God has a solution to both the victim and the violator.

Tip

The term "abuse" covers a broad spectrum of behaviors and actions, thus making it difficult to define. The four types of abuse are: emotional, psychological, verbal and physical. Notice what Colossians 1:13 says – *"[The Father] has delivered and drawn us to Himself out of the control and the dominion of darkness and has transferred us into the kingdom of the Son of His love." (AMPC)* Satan is the author of abuse, and as new creations we neither have to be under his control in abusing our spouse, nor in being abused by our spouse. Christ has set us free. Deal with the abuse immediately and let the Holy Spirit and godly counsel guide you into what is appropriate to your situation. Whatever we do to one another, we are doing to a member of the body of Christ. Repent and seek counsel in dealing with whatever is driving you to abuse or to accept abuse.

Scripture

[The Father] has delivered and drawn us to Himself out of control and the dominion of darkness and has transferred us into the kingdom of the Son of His love, in Whom we have our redemption through His blood, [which means] the forgiveness of our sins. (Colossians 1:13-14 AMPC)

Exercise

Research abuse and become familiar with the four types of abuse mentioned in the tip. Talk about the issue of abuse in your relationship, whether small or large. If you are dealing with warning signs of abuse, seek counsel immediately and make the necessary changes to cease in abusing or receiving abuse. (Obviously, if you feel threatened you may need to call 911. Pray after you are free from danger.)

Affirmation

We have the Greater One living inside of us. God did not give us the spirit of abuse but the spirit of love, patience and long-suffering. As a loving couple we will not allow our differences to ever escalate to emotional, psychological, verbal or physical abuse. Abuse is demonic and we are children of God; therefore, we will not allow any member of our body to be abusive to our spouse. Satan is the author of abuse, and as a new creation we will not allow the spirit of abuse to step foot in our marriage relationship. We are *not* under the control of Satan. Satan is *not* lord over our life. We declare that Colossians 1:13-14 is in operation in our marriage – *"[The Father] has delivered and drawn us to Himself out of the control and the dominion of darkness and has transferred us into the kingdom of the Son of His love, in Whom we have our redemption through His blood, [which means] the forgiveness of our sins." (AMPC)* We will seek outside help to help us navigate through trauma from past hurts.

Prayer

Father, we delight in your love and your power. We are your children wrapped under your wings of protection. No weapon formed against us will prosper and every tongue that exalts itself against us shall be condemned. We have everything we need to be successful, so we will not allow ourselves to walk recklessly and be abusive and out of control. Father, anoint us with the power of your Hoy Spirit and remove from us fits of rage, anger, wrath and strife. We repent and turn away from following after demonic, dark, abusive behavior. Lord, remove from us corrupt thinking towards our spouse that would provoke us to negative thinking that prompts us to yield to violence. We vow to never allow satanic thoughts, words and imaginations to ever control our life. You have not given us a spirit of abuse, anger and rage, but you have given us your Holy Spirit. We break the power of darkness trying to operate in our marriage in the area abuse. We have you, the Greater One, living inside of us, and we are overcomers. We submit and yield to the power of your Spirit. Anoint us and empower us resist the devil and turn away from abuse. In your name we pray! Amen!

Week 49

Sexual Abuse

Sexual abuse, a very complex form of abuse, is not necessarily a category alone but rather is a combination of physical, psychological and emotional abuse.

Tip

Sexual abuse may be present in the following ways:

- Anger or jealousy,
- Criticism sexually,
- Withholding sex or affection to hurt or punish someone,
- Publicly showing interest in others,
- Forcing unwanted sexual acts or forcing sex after beating, or
- Forcing any part of sex using guilt, coercion, or manipulation.

Sexual intimacy is something that God your heavenly Father created. Let's face it; God created the sexual organs to experience orgasm. So it's certainly God's will for you to have a wonderful sexual experience with your spouse. However, anything that God creates for good, the devil wants to pervert its use and destroy lives in the process. So sexual abuse is clearly of Satan and his kingdom. "... *For the devil has sinned (violated the divine law) from the be-*

ginning. The reason the Son of God was made manifest (visible) was to undo (destroy, loosen, and dissolve) the works the devil [has done]." (1 John 3:8b AMPC) Since Jesus came to destroy and loose us from the works of the devil, these verses also include sexual abuse designed to distort God's design of sex. Thank God, for we are free today!

Scripture

[But] he who commits sin [who practices evildoing] is of the devil [takes his character from the evil one], for the devil has sinned (violated the divine law) from the beginning. The reason the Son of God was made manifest (visible) was to undo (destroy, loosen, and dissolve) the works the devil [has done]. (1 John 3:8 AMPC)

Exercise

Have an open discussion about sex. Here are some questions:

- What was your exposure to sex like growing up?
- Did you experience any abuse, violation or trauma regarding sex?
- When did you have your first sexual experience?
- When did you become aware of God's commandment regarding sex?
- What picture did your church or ministry paint of sex?
- How do you view sex today?
- How would you like to view sexual intimacy?

- Do you feel you have any sexual hang-ups or dysfunctions?
- How do you feel about the sex we experience as a couple?

Affirmation

Thank you, Father, that we have deep, passionate, steaming sexual intimacy with one another. You created sex to be pleasurable and enjoyable. Sexual intimacy is something that you created, Father, for us to enjoy with one another intimately. We are free from sexual abuse in our marriage union. We allow the help of the Holy Spirit to help us be open with one another to discuss areas where we have been sexually abused by family members or others in our lifetime. Not discussing rape, violation or molestation will only hinder our sexual intimacy together. We purpose to love each other passionately, intimately, not withholding and not dodging one another.

Father you created our sex organs to experience orgasms in order for us to enjoy the pleasure of our *holy union*. Sexual intimacy draws us closer together in love and understanding one another, so we purpose to come together sexually and enjoy orgasms as often as we can. As a Christian woman I will not withhold and become weird concerning having sex with my spouse. I am excited and I look forward to sharing our love together. As a husband I am not impatient, forceful or condemning when it comes to intimacy with my spouse. We pray and ask God to open our hearts and minds to discuss areas of sexual abuse. We will not be ashamed or embarrassed about our past violations. We welcome the opportunity to be set free. Our sexual intimacy is frequent, often, pleasurable, steamy, loving and enjoyable. We don't look for ways to stop having sex with each other, but we look for ways to engage in sexual intimacy on a regular basis.

Prayer

Father, thank you for creating sex to be pleasurable and enjoyable. Father, you gave us sexual organs so we could have orgasm, which is very satisfying. Thank you, Father, that we are free from sexual abuse of past relationships and traumatic incidents of sexual abuse. Father, we desire to be complete and fully free to love each other. We will not allow rape, molestation or sexual abuse to control our present and future intimacy with one another. Bring healing and wholeness to us as individuals and in areas where we have been violated sexually. We release bitterness, unforgiveness and resentment for what we've encountered through sexual abuse. Jesus, when you were on the cross you said, Father, forgive them, for they do not know what they are doing. So we say today, Lord, we forgive our sexual attackers from what they did to us, because they were under the control of demons and they did not know what they were doing. Lord, heal us from any hang-ups, quirks, being inhibited sexually and inability to move forward in our sexual intimacy because of the abuse. Your Word says, *"Whoever's sins you forgive, they are forgiven them. Whoever's sins you retain, they have been retained." (John 20:23 WEB)* We release today all the sins that have been committed against us sexually from the time we were children until this present day. We release them out of our heart.

Father God, thank you for teaching us that holding on to any sins only makes the sin occur over and over again in our life. We are free from the effects of sexual abuse, and we are free to fully engage in sexual intimacy frequently, having sex as often as possible. Father God, give us a fresh release to be more passionate and intimate than ever before. In Jesus' name, amen.

Week 50

Past Relationships

Past relationships can have a negative impact on the present marriage union.

Tip

Everybody has a past. Some have a more "checkered" past than others.

God can heal and God can restore our emotions. The problem is people assume just because they are no longer with the person, it is over and they can just move on. This can be denial. First you must address any issue of pain and hurt through forgiveness. If you don't, your current spouse will feel the residue of that negativity. Next, you must close the door completely to old relationships. Unless you have children together, there is no need to be in communication with them. If there are children involved, it is important that your spouse stays in the loop of *all communications and all interactions*. This is whether your ex likes it or not. Also, be sure not to allow yourself to be manipulated by what control your ex may exert regarding the children. Some exes have no problem using the children for devious means. What is important here is that you are married to your spouse. This is the most important relationship you have right now—even more important than your children. Your children's best opportunity for support they need from you will occur when you are experiencing a healthy and fulfilling marriage. So, keep first things first.

Scripture

Brothers, I do not consider that I have made it my own. But one thing I do: forgetting what lies behind and straining forward to what lies ahead, I press on toward the goal for the prize of the upward call of God in Christ Jesus. (Philippians 3:13-14)

Exercise

Be open about any past issues that are affecting you now. Walk through the healing process together. As you uncover the unresolved issue, you may feel emotions about it. Think of it like peeling an onion. Issues tend to manifest one layer at a time. Be sure and allow God to make you whole, so you can freely and completely love your spouse today.

Affirmation

We are free from past relationships that have a negative impact upon our marriage. We will search our heart to forgive and release every person with whom we have had a negative experience. We will not have times in our life where we are so angry when we think about a past relationship, because we are dealing with the unforgiveness and bitterness now. We say to past relationships that had a negative impact emotionally on our life, we release you from controlling our life. Thank you, Father, for you are *Jehovah Rapha*, the Lord who heals us. We submit to the healing process concerning past relationships. We choose not to live in the past and be dominated by the impact it can bring. We stand on your Word in Philippians 3:13-14, *"Brothers, I do not consider that I have made it my own. But one thing I do: forgetting what lies behind and straining forward to what lies ahead, I press on toward the goal for the prize of the upward call of God in Christ Jesus." (ESV)* As a couple we are moving more and more into a brighter day for giving up things that are past and pressing towards the things that are present.

Prayer

"But as it is written: 'Eye has not seen, nor ear heard, nor have entered into the heart of man the things which God has prepared for those who love Him.' But God has revealed them to us through His Spirit. For the Spirit searches all things, yes, the deep things of God." (1 Corinthians 2:9-10 NKJV).

Father, thank you for preparing great and wonderful things for us as a couple. There are things we have not seen with our eyes nor heard with our ears nor have entered into our heart what you are doing. We rejoice and delight in the gift you are preparing for us as a couple. We ask that you would bring healing in our hearts as individuals and as a couple so that our connection with one another will be smoother and our love will be deeper and not hindered from issues in past relationships. We thank you, Father, for giving us the capacity and ability to forgive past relationships and hurts. We will not allow the past to dominate and control our future relationship with each other. Thank you for pouring out your healing oil in our hearts, minds and emotions concerning the pain of past relationships. We will not retain sins of bitterness and negative thoughts concerning past relationships. We put it all under the blood of Jesus Christ. We will not live our life in the past and be dominated by the past. Thank you, Father, for purging our minds from past hurts and sweeping us fast into the future. Thank you, Father, that only goodness and mercy are following us every day of our life.

Week 51

Love one another

Mastering the love walk is the single most important pursuit in your relationship.

Tip

Unconditional love cannot be talked about enough. It is love that will create a culture of compassion, forgiveness, forbearance and deep intimacy. The more you grow in love, the deeper you will understand the Father and the more access you will have to the power of God working in your behalf. Your prayers will be answered quicker, you will overcome offense faster, and the more complete healing you will experience when you are hurt through a conflict. So love your spouse through the love of God inside of you.

Scripture

I give you a new commandment: that you should love one another. Just as I have loved you, so you too should love one another. (John 13:34 AMPC)

Exercise

Review the love passage below and examine each portion of the verses to see how you can improve in your love walk.

"Love endures long and is patient and kind; love never is envious nor boils over with jealousy, is not boastful or vainglorious, does not display itself haughtily.

"It is not conceited (arrogant and inflated with pride); it is not rude (unmannerly) and does not act unbecomingly. Love (God's love in us) does not insist on its own rights or its own way, for it is not self-seeking; it is not touchy or fretful or resentful; it takes no account of the evil done to it [it pays no attention to a suffered wrong].

"It does not rejoice at injustice and unrighteousness, but rejoices when right and truth prevail.

"Love bears up under anything and everything that comes, is ever ready to believe the best of every person, its hopes are fadeless under all circumstances, and it endures everything [without weakening].

"Love never fails [never fades out or becomes obsolete or comes to an end]." (1 Corinthians 13:4-8 AMPC)

Next, meditate on this passage in the morning and evening by reading it out loud and asking the Holy Spirit to assist in living out the scripture. Lastly, look for a "love project" to grow your love in. A love project is something about your spouse that "gets on your nerves." Learn to love them until it no longer bothers you. This is assuming it is not destructive to the future of your relationship together. This is generally referring to personality traits and idiosyncrasies.

Affirmation

As a couple we will love one another for love is from God. *"Beloved, let us love one another, for love is from God, and whoever loves has been born of God and knows God. Anyone who does not love does not know God, because God is love." (1 John 4:7-8 ESV)* We decree that my spouse and I are walking in the love of God with each other. We confess 1 Corinthians 13:4-8, *"Love endures long and is patient and kind; love never is envious nor boils over with jealousy, is not boastful or vainglorious, does not display itself haughtily. It is not conceited (arrogant and inflated with pride); it is not rude (unmannerly) and does not act unbecomingly. Love (God's love in us) does not insist on its own rights or its own way, for it is not self-seeking; it is not touchy or fretful or resentful; it takes no account of the evil done to it [it pays no attention to a suffered wrong]. It does not rejoice at injustice and unrighteousness but rejoices when right and truth prevail. Love bears up under anything, and everything that comes, is ever ready to believe the best of every person, its hopes are fadeless under all circumstances, and it endures everything [without weakening]. Love never fails [never fades out or becomes obsolete or comes to an end]." (AMPC)* We will love one another and are taking quality time to master the love walk with each other. We strive to operate in unconditional love. This will create a culture of compassion, forgiveness, forbearance and deep intimacy for one another.

Prayer

"For God so loved the world that he gave his one and only Son, that whoever believes in him shall not perish but have eternal life." (John 3:16 NIV) Father, you sent Jesus here on this earth to deliver us and set us free from the works of the devil, but you also sent him to teach us how to walk in love. We will follow after the footsteps of Jesus and dedicate our lives to walk in loving one another with our whole heart. Father God, develop in us love that endures long and is patient and kind. Help us to become bigger than our issues and immaturities. Lord, show us how to be patient and long-suffering with each other as husband and wife. Lord, we ask that you remove areas from us that are conceited, arrogant and inflated with pride because, Lord, that is not the love of God. Lord, thank you that we do not insist on our own rights or our own way. Father God, help us not to be selfish and self-seeking, touchy, fretful and resentful. Lord, help us not to take account of suffered wrongs against each other. God is love and so, Father, we are going to follow in your footsteps and be people of love. Then our prayers will be answered quicker, we will overcome offense faster and we will experience more complete healing when we are hurt through a conflict.

Week 52

Adultery

If your spouse has committed adultery and you decide to work through the pain of betrayal and distrust, God can completely heal and restore your marriage.

Tip

Adultery causes a tremendous amount of pain, leaves a stain on your marriage and is very difficult to overcome due to a few factors:

1. Trust is broken, and it is hard to earn it back.
2. Condemnation from others, your spouse or the enemy can almost be overwhelming. (We define condemnation as experiencing guilt from past repented sins.)
3. Insecurity from your spouse. They gave you their heart before and you crushed it. So what will happen to them if you do it again?
4. How was this sin exposed?
    - Did you confess?
    - Were you caught in a lie?
    - Is this a one-time experience or multiple times, multiple years or multiple sexual partners?
5. Your spouse committed adultery because they wanted to hurt you back.

All these issues are like unscrambling eggs! You can't do it by yourself. Seek professional help from someone who has been restored from a similar experience. You will need to restart your courtship and rebuild your covenant with each other and with God over time. Know that he can and will restore what was lost!

Scripture

If we [freely] admit that we have sinned and confessed our sins, He is faithful and just (true to His own nature and promises) and will forgive our sins [dismiss our lawlessness] and [continuously] cleanse us from all unrighteousness [everything not in conformity to His will and purpose, thought, and action]. (1 John 1:9 AMPC)

Exercise

If you are committed to rebuilding your broken covenant, sit down and talk about why you are choosing to stay in the marriage and move forward. Write down your "why." Discuss the challenges you have to move forward. Seek professional help and submit your answers to them. Follow their advice and be accountable to their instructions.

Affirmation

If my spouse has committed adultery, I know that God can heal us through the pain and restore our marriage. We observe 1 John 1:9 – *"If we [freely] admit that we have sinned and confess our sins, He is faithful and just (true to*

His own nature and promises) and will forgive our sins [dismiss our lawlessness] and [continuously] cleanse us from all unrighteousness [everything not in conformity to His will in purpose, thought, and action]." (AMPC) We are determined that nothing will destroy our marriage. We confess the sin of adultery to our spouse and ask for complete forgiveness from them. We know God will, and we know it will take time to heal the pain that we experience, but we will stand in faith together as God heals us. We will sit down and talk about why we are choosing to stay in the marriage and move forward. We will discuss the challenges we are having in moving forward. We will seek professional help to navigate us to a place of harmony in our marriage again. We will trust in the Lord with all our heart to restore, heal and bring us to complete unity again. We will shut every door that was open that calls us to commit adultery.

Prayer

Father, thank you that you will never leave us nor forsake us, because you are our God. We stand on your Word – *"The LORD is near to those who are discouraged; he saves those who have lost all hope." (Psalm 34:18 GNT)* Father, we repent for sinning against you and each other in the area of committing adultery. We will submit ourselves to you and resist the devil—he will flee from us. We thank you, Father, for shutting every door that let adultery into our marriage. We have damaged our marriage to a great extent, but we are committed to rebuilding our broken covenant. Surround us with your presence of peace, love and compassion as we sit down and asked why we are staying in our marriage. Give us the strength to love and forgive each other. We will not focus on the negativity that comes from the offense of adultery, but we will focus on rebuilding the love in our marriage. Father, help us to overcome issues of trust and condemnation from others and ourselves. Free us from guilt and insecurity because of the adultery that occurred in our marriage. Enlarge our heart and our mind so that we can seek to understand and to listen and to hear when our spouses are sharing. Because adultery has bought a tremendous amount of pain in our marriage, we need you to heal our heart completely, purge out this deep pain and restore us. Open our eyes so we can see the love we once had and strive to reach towards loving again. Father, please give us the power to move past this place in our life. We are moving towards happy, harmonious marriage goals. Satan is defeated, and Jesus is Lord.

A Marriage Investment Story . . .

Maybe the Lord did not speak to me?

"I planted, Apollos watered, but God gave the growth." (1 Corinthians 3:6 ESV)

I was going through a very dark time in my life a few years ago. When you are a results-driven person like me, you can get frustrated when things are not happening as planned. I worked very hard to build my local ministry, and things were not happening according to my schedule. So, I began to doubt whether or not God really spoke to me. I began to question my vision. "Maybe the desire to build a ministry was just my imagination. Maybe God never really spoke to me in the first place. Maybe the call on my life wasn't what I thought it to be." I was deeply discouraged.

I have been discouraged before, but I think in that season of my life, it was probably the worst. I remember sitting on my bed saying to Sandra that I didn't believe God had spoken to me: "After all, I am a failure; I have not produced fruit; if God were with me I would be successful!" My Sandra grabbed my hands, and she got really close in my face like a trainer in a boxer's corner after he had taken a beating. Sandra said to me with her face almost touching my face, "NO! NO! I remember when God spoke to you. I was there! You did not fail; you did not miss God! You are not a failure. You will finish what you started. I won't let you quit. I am with you. We will succeed together." I wept like a baby.

Sandra's encouraging words are the reason I am so strong and vibrant today. We all need a person who believes in us and will finish the journey with us. That's why marriage can be so powerful. Remember the words of Solomon:

"Two are better than one, because they have a good reward for their toil. For if they fall, one will lift up his fellow. But woe to him who is alone when he falls and has not another to lift him up! Again, if two lie together, they keep warm, but how can one keep warm alone? And though a man might prevail against one who is alone, two will withstand him—a threefold cord is not quickly broken." (Ecclesiastes 4:9-12 ESV)

Through Sandra's strong words of encouragement, I was able to shake off my "stinking thinking." I was able to look inside and draw out the strength I have in the person of the Holy Spirit and press forward. Our job is to plant and water, but only God can make things grow. My perspective was skewed, and Sandra helped me get my fire back.

If I spent our relationship beating Sandra down with my words and being critical, she would not be able to build me up and encourage me when I needed help. Also, if I did everything alone, and never communicated my vision, she would be out of the loop and unable to affirm what I said and hold me accountable to what I believed God was saying to me. God knew what he was doing when he brought us together.

As we begin this new venture of impacting couples through this resource, we look forward to building together. Sandra and I cannot guarantee we will never want to quit and never be discouraged, but we can guarantee that we will never allow ourselves to be discouraged and want to quit on the same day! We are better than that, and our God is with us always! It is our prayer that this resource will inspire, encourage and empower you to grow deeper in your love for one another and grow stronger in your connection with Jesus as the shepherd and bishop of your sacred union!

"For this reason a man shall leave [behind] his father and his mother and be joined to his wife and cleave closely to her permanently, and the two shall become one flesh, so that they are no longer two, but one flesh What therefore God has united (joined together), let not man separate or divide." (Mark 10:7-9 AMPC)

BONUS WEEK! This is the most important week ever!

Date nights

It is so easy to get married, enjoy your honeymoon, get back to work, have children, take your kids to school, help them with homework, take care of them when they are sick, take them to sports events, special clubs, church activities, serve in several positions at church, at your kids school, participate in community events, and . . .

You look up a few years later and you hardly know each other, let alone take the time to date! Who has the money, time and energy? But if you don't take the time to date each other and put this activity above everything else you are doing, chances are you will grow apart and fall out of love and become roommates, drivers and chaperones for your kids. When your kids are grown and on their own, you will have nothing in common but will continue to live with each other in your dead relationship. You will most likely get another spouse, or just stay together as roommates until you die. You will probably stop having sex and look forward to the day when *that* is over! So sad! And so, so pitiful! God has something better!

Tip

Date night is the most important activity in your marriage. Why? Because what you did to *get* her/him, you need to do to *keep* her/him. Make date night a SACRED time for each other. Don't allow anything to make you cancel! Let everyone know—friends, relatives, kids, church members, business partners and associates, your job (if you have that type of freedom). Once you set it in your schedule, it becomes a part of how you function in your relationship. Everyone in our circle of relationships knows John and Sandra's weekly date day. It happens to be Friday. There are those times due to travel and emergencies when it is impossible to keep our day, but we make up for the day earlier in the week or a day or so after. We started with once per month, then biweekly and now weekly. Spend money, look good and enjoy yourselves! (Really dress up sometimes.)

Scripture

May your fountain be blessed, and may you rejoice in your young wife—a loving doe, a graceful deer; may her breasts satisfy you at all times, may you be captivated by her love always. (Proverbs 5:18-19 NET Bible)

Note: The positive instruction is now given: Find pleasure in a fulfilling marriage. The "fountain" is another in the series of implied comparisons with the sexual pleasure that must be fulfilled at home. That it should be blessed (the passive participle of *barakh*) indicates that sexual delight is God-given; having it blessed would mean that it would be endowed with fruitfulness, that it would fulfill all that God intended it to do. (N39 NET Bible First Edition Notes)

He brought me to the banqueting house, and his banner over me was love. (Songs of Solomon 2:4 ESV)

Exercise

Set a specific time to go out on a date. This can start once per month, twice per month or weekly. This can eventually become a date *day*. We have practiced having a date day for many decades. We like to start in the morning for breakfast. After breakfast we spend the entire day doing something we love. So make sure you keep it fun and flexible. Plan sometimes but sometimes just go with it! Turn off your phone, put away your work. Ditch the kids! This is one time when you can have some hot steamy sex for sho! Rent a hotel room sometimes so you don't have to be quiet!

Affirmation

Heavenly Father, we declare that your banner over our relationship is love. We truly love each other; we truly value each other. We delight in each other! We choose to make our date time together the most sacred part of our holy union. It is our desire to show true love for one another as we build a deeper bond and an intimate connection. Father we declare that you are in the midst of our time together, enabling us to free our hearts from the cares of this life and rejoice in this special time! We are important enough to set time aside to cultivate our love for each other always!

Prayer

Father, we approach your throne in the name of Jesus, prince of peace and true redeemer. Adam and Eve were cursed because of their sin and lost connection with you. That lost connection formed a breach in their ability to fulfill your design for marriage. The effects of the curse are still present to this very day. But Jesus not only restored and reconnected us to you, our heavenly Father, but his presence on earth, particularly his death, burial and resurrection, restored our ability to have a successful and fulfilling relationship with you and with one another. Today we ask your blessing on our date times. *Jehovah Jireh*, provide the resources for us to really enjoy ourselves. Provide the time and the peace in our circumstances to date each other without distractions. And when the day is complete, bless our marriage bed with great sex! You provide such a blessing for your son and daughter. Thank you, Father, for we know that you rejoice over us and it pleases you that we live out your design. Lord, may we live out what you had in your mind when you created this thing called marriage! In Jesus the Christ's name, AMEN! And AMEN!

Biographies

John and Sandra Posey (married 39 years) bring a distinct mix of ministry, business and leadership to a number of diverse communities. They have served in multiple, social, ethnic, technical, religious and educational communities with a combined experience of 80 years. John and Sandra complement each other as a team to provide solutions to a vast range of spiritual, personal, business, ministry and relational issues. They desire to shorten the learning curve for couples and encourage them to work toward God's one-flesh idea, so their prayers are not hindered. With unhindered prayer anything is possible! Total peace and unity in their covenant relationship will give couples access to God's supernatural math. *"One will chase a thousand and two will put ten thousand to flight!" (Deuteronomy 32:30, adapted)* In other words, with God working in a marriage union, one plus one equals ten! Many couples spend so much energy fighting over petty issues until all of their thought, gifts and talent power are canceled out (one minus one equals zero). Why? Because God will not bless mess!

John has earned an Electrical Engineering degree and a doctorate in Pastoral Theology, and Sandra is currently working on her masters in Christian Counseling. They are marriage and life coaches, and provide training, mentoring and leadership development in many environments and communities.

John and Sandra are members in good standing with

the Righteous Preachers Network, 7000 More Covenant Churches and Ministries, RHEMA Ministerial Association International, and the International Ministers Fellowship. They have taken numerous courses, classes and workshops earning certificates and certifications, ranging from business management and leadership to life coaching and streaming media consulting. They believe the key to fulfilling your dreams is to grow into them. Lastly, John holds a fifth-degree black belt (master level), and Sandra holds a red belt in Moo Duk Kwan, Tang Soo Do Martial Arts with the National Black Belt Karate Association.

John and Sandra served as the founding pastors of Zoe Christian Fellowship for 25 years and are Co-Founders of the Zoe City House Church Movement in the greater Atlanta Area. House Churches mobilize authentic Christ followers to take the gospel of Jesus into today's marketplace. John is the Area Director of the Christian Business Men's Connection of Atlanta (an organization founded in 1930, with a global footprint of 300+ cities in the U.S. and 98 countries). John and Sandra are the founders of Marriage Equity Systems, a marriage life coaching, training and mentoring organization whose mission is to train and equip couples to "INVEST IN LOVE FOR A LIFETIME RETURN."

Family Life

John and Sandra are the proud parents of three daughters: Rhea, Tasha and Alexus, and VERY proud grandparents of Zoe Alexandria Saunders.

Let's take another step and make a deeper connection with John and Sandra!

Visit www.MarriageEquitySystems.com and join our VIP List! Here's why!

1. Receive up-to-date content to strengthen your love for one another!
2. Get "sneak peek" access to the greatest and latest, hot-off-the-press insight from John and Sandra's marriage treasure chest. (A lot of stuff in there!)
3. First opportunity for discounts to special events and resources as they become available!

Download the Marriage Equity mobile app for your mobile device.

This PWA (progressive web app) will not take up any storage space on your mobile device. Download it now by going to app.marriageequtitysystems.com and gain instant access to resources, videos, articles, social media and much, much more!

Join the MARRIAGE EQUITY CLUB at an introductory price!

Bronze Level $29/mo.

- Private account with user name and password
- Additional video content on one of the 52-week devotional subject matter updated regularly
- Access to a monthly webinar hosted by John and Sandra Posey
- Monthly tips about how to best use our 52-week devotional

Silver Level $59/mo.

Bronze Level PLUS . . .

- Access to 1 Mastermind marriage team hosted by John and Sandra on 52-Week Marriage devotional Best Practices
- One "private" marriage coaching session with John and Sandra per year

Gold Level $99/mo.

Silver Level PLUS . . .

- 1 additional Marriage mastermind team taking a deep dive into our 52-Week Marriage Devotional
- 1 additional private marriage coaching session with John and Sandra per year
- 5 Additional Devotional Subjects created by your mastermind team
- An overcoming the ISSUE assessment analysis
- Sneak Peak into John and Sandra's Next Book "Overcoming THE issue: The one flesh barrier"
- Additional Discounts on all events and resources
- Invitation to become a Marriage Equity Systems Coach by John and Sandra

Platinum Level $250/mo.

Gold Level PLUS . . .

- One private coaching session with John and Sandra every six weeks
- Free access to all events and resources under $500
- Special discounts for events over $500
- Discounted Marriage Equity Systems Coach Training by John and Sandra

Take advantage of our INTRODUCTORY price offerings and be first to "invest in love for a lifetime return"!

Notes

Notes

Notes

Made in USA - Kendallville, IN
73767_9781733795906
08.19.2022 1421